REF
500

Kingfisher Science
Encyclopedia
(Vol. 10)

6277

KINGFISHER
SCIENCE
ENCYCLOPEDIA

KINGFISHER
SCIENCE
ENCYCLOPEDIA

General Editor: Catherine Headlam

10

ULTRAHIGH FREQUENCY
ZYGOTE

Kingfisher Books

Kingfisher Books, Grisewood & Dempsey Ltd
Elsley House, 24–30 Great Titchfield Street,
London W1P 7AD

First published in 1991 by Kingfisher Books

Library of Congress Cataloging-in-Publication Data available.

ISBN 0 86272 853 3

Printed in Italy

GENERAL EDITOR
Catherine Headlam

EDITORIAL DIRECTOR
Jim Miles

ASSISTANT EDITORS
Lee Simmons
Charlotte Evans

EDITORIAL ASSISTANT
Andrea Moran

CONSULTANTS
Professor Lawrence F. Lowery, University of California, Berkeley, USA
Alison Porter, Education Officer, Science Museum, London

EDUCATIONAL CONSULTANTS
Terry Cash, Coordinator of a team of advisory teachers in Essex
Robert Pressling, Math Coordinator,
Hillsgrove Primary School, London

CONTRIBUTORS
Joan Angelbeck
Michael Chinery
John Clark
Neil Curtis
Gwen Edmonds
Andrew Fisher
William Gould
Ian Graham
William Hemsley
James Muirden
John Paton
Brian Ward
Wendy Wasels
Peter Way

DESIGN
Ralph Pitchford
Allan Hardcastle
Ross George
Judy Crammond

PICTURE RESEARCH
Tim Russell
Elaine Willis

PRODUCTION
Dawn Hickman

FOREWORD

When the 21st century dawns, science, mathematics, and accompanying technologies will be deeply interwoven within the fabric of all societies. The scientifically literate citizen of the next century will be the person who: knows that science, mathematics, and technology are interdependent human enterprises with strengths and limitations; understands key concepts and principles within the grand conceptual frameworks of science; is familiar with the natural world and recognizes both its diversity and unity; uses scientific knowledge and scientific ways of thinking for individual and social purposes.

Today's youngsters will be tomorrow's citizens and leaders. They will make decisions that will affect the quality of the world environment and the quality of life on this planet. To prepare for tomorrow, today's youngsters must have access to the knowledge of science early in their lives — when there is a budding interest and broad general curiosity about many topics. What better way to provide this knowledge than through a storehouse of scientific and technological information in the form of an encyclopedia written in a manner appropriate to beginning levels of interest? Never before has such a resource been provided. Prepared in the spirit and character of scientific inquiry and integrated with scientific values, the *Kingfisher Science Encyclopedia* provides more than facts. It invites youngsters to actively hypothesize by posing challenging questions, to collect and use evidence through suggested investigations, and to explore new topics that subsequently interrelate and extend ideas. It places a premium on the natural curiosity and creativity of youngsters. And it provides them with the challenges and issues that the future must face.

The contents of the *Kingfisher Science Encyclopedia* is the work of many people — those who compiled the information as well as those who discovered the ideas. It is a work of love and care for the purpose of contributing to an enlightened citizenry that will live most of its life in the next century.

Professor Lawrence F. Lowery
Graduate School of Education
and the Lawrence Hall of Science
University of California
Berkeley, California

SAFETY CODE

Some science experiments can be dangerous. Ask an adult to help you with difficult hammering or cutting and any experiments that involve flames, hot liquids, or chemicals. Do not forget to put out any flames and turn off the heat when you have finished. Good scientists avoid accidents.

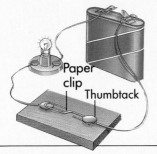

Paper clip

Thumbtack

Wide rubber band

Brass paper clip

ELECTRICITY
- Never use electricity from the outlet for experiments.
- Use batteries for all experiments that need electricity. Dispose of batteries carefully when they are used up and never heat them up or take them apart.

HEATING
- Tie back hair and be careful of loose clothes.
- Only heat small quantities of a substance.
- Always have an adult with you.
- Never heat any container with a top on it. Always point what you are heating away from you.
- Never hold something in your hands to heat it. Use a holder that does not conduct heat.

SAFE SOURCES OF HEAT
- Hot water from the faucet is a good source of heat.
- A hair dryer can be used to dry things. Always take care when using electricity near water.

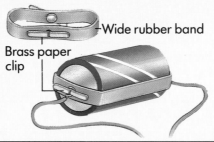

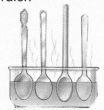

Sand

Metal tray

- For direct heat use a short thick candle placed in sand in a metal tray.

CHEMICALS AND QUANTITIES
- Only use a small amount of any substance even if it is just salt or vinegar.
- Never taste or eat chemicals
- Clean up all spillages immediately, especially if on your skin.
- Wash your hands after using chemicals.
- Always ask an adult before using any substance; many cooking or cleaning substances used at home are very powerful.
- Smell chemicals very carefully. Do not breathe in deeply any strong smells.
- Never handle chemicals with your bare hands. Use an old spoon and wash it very carefully after use.
- Label **all** chemicals.

SUN
- Never look directly at the Sun, especially when using a telescope or binoculars.

PLANTS AND ANIMALS
- Never pick wild flowers.
- Collect insects carefully so as not to harm them. Release them afterward.
- Be careful of stinging insects.

SAFE CONTAINERS
- Use plastic containers if an experiment does not require heating or strong chemicals.
- Use heat-proof glass or metal containers if you are using heat.
- Avoid using ordinary glass as it may shatter.

CUTTING
- Use scissors rather than a knife whenever possible.
- When using a knife keep your fingers behind the cutting edge.
- Put what you are cutting on a board that will not slip and will prevent damage to the surface underneath.

Ultrahigh frequency (UHF)

Ultrahigh frequency (UHF) is the name given to ELEC-TROMAGNETIC RADIATION which has an even higher FREQUENCY than VERY HIGH FREQUENCY (VHF) radio waves. A UHF wave has a frequency between 300 and 3,000 megahertz (a MHz is one million cycles per second). Because of its frequency, a UHF radio wave can carry much more information every second than an ordinary radio wave or a VHF signal. For example, UHF radio waves are used to broadcast TELEVISION signals. These contain a great deal of information because one of three colors has to be given to each spot on the screen each time the beam of the CATHODE-RAY TUBE in the television set passes over it. Hundreds of thousands of spots are scanned 25 or 30 times every second, so tens of millions of pieces of information have to be carried.

UHF signals are used to communicate with artificial SATELLITES and other spacecraft. They allow a lot of information to be transferred and they can pass easily through the IONOSPHERE, the layer of the upper ATMOSPHERE that reflects ordinary radio waves.

Television and radio waves

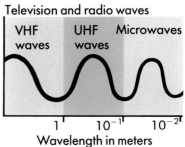

▲ Ultrahigh frequency waves have frequencies greater than very high frequency waves but lower than microwaves.

◀ UHF waves travel in straight lines and pass through all the layers of the Earth's atmosphere without being bent or reflected (unlike radio waves of lower frequencies). They are used to send telephone messages, television signals, and computer data over long distances via communications satellites.

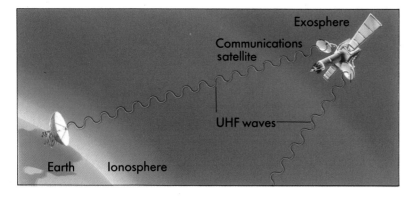

Ultrasound

Ultrasound is SOUND that cannot be heard because its FREQUENCY is greater than the highest frequency that the human EAR can detect. Sound with a frequency greater than 20 kilohertz (a kHz is one thousand cycles per second) can be described as ultrasound or ultrasonic. Ultrasound has a wide variety of uses. If the sound vibrations are strong enough, they can shake objects clean. If a dirty object is dipped into water and the ultrasound is switched on, the dirt is vibrated loose and falls from the object. The vibrations can also be used to break

An ultrasonic wave passed through a liquid or a solid makes the liquid or solid vibrate at a very fast rate. These vibrations can be used to mix paint thoroughly, clean tools, and homogenize milk by breaking up the fat particles. In dentistry, a drill controlled by ultrasonic vibrations can penetrate tooth enamel with very little friction or heat.

▶ An ultrasound scanner builds up a picture of an unborn baby in its mother's womb. This technique, which is painless for the mother and harmless for the baby, is used to check the progress of pregnancy.

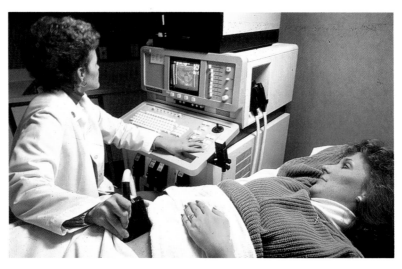

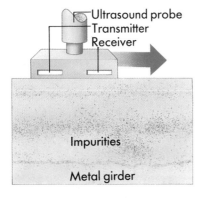

Ultrasound probe
Transmitter
Receiver

Impurities

Metal girder

▲ Ultrasound scanning is used to detect flaws and impurities in metals. The ultrasound probe is moved along the surface of the metal to be tested. The probe has a transmitter to produce ultrasound and a receiver to detect it. The main reflections, or echoes, come from the top and bottom surfaces. But any impurities also reflect the ultrasonic waves and show up as a trace on a screen or print-out.

▶ The eyes of some insects, such as bees, are sensitive to ultraviolet light. To a bee, these lobelia flowers look dark with pale lines down the middle of the petals. This encourages it to visit the flowers and pollinate them. Humans cannot see these lines (right) because in visible light the petals appear pale all over.

up painful growths in the kidneys called kidney stones.

Ultrasound can be used to reveal details that cannot normally be seen. Ships and submarines have SONAR systems that use ultrasound to "see" under water. Scanners used in hospitals to check on the progress of unborn babies also use ultrasound. A scanner transmits ultrasound into the mother's body and receives reflections from inside. The reflections are displayed as a picture on a screen. Ultrasound is used because it is safer for the developing baby than X-rays.

Ultraviolet radiation

Ultraviolet radiation is ELECTROMAGNETIC RADIATION which has a higher FREQUENCY than the LIGHT we can see. It lies beyond the blue or violet end of the visible SPECTRUM. Each PHOTON (particle) of ultraviolet light carries more ENERGY than photons of visible light, so

MOLECULES which absorb ultraviolet radiation receive a large amount of energy. This extra energy can cause the molecule to break apart. This means that CHEMICAL REACTIONS can take place in ultraviolet light which would not otherwise occur. Ultraviolet light in sunlight can cause people's skin to burn. Large amounts of ultraviolet radiation can be dangerous. The OZONE LAYER is important because it absorbs most of the ultraviolet radiation from the Sun before it reaches the Earth. *See also* INFRARED RADIATION; PHOTOCHEMISTRY.

Universe

The universe is the whole of space and everything in it. Astronomers believe that it was formed after the BIG BANG, which probably took place about 15 billion years ago. The universe has been expanding ever since, and the clusters of GALAXIES in it (including the cluster containing the MILKY WAY, where our SOLAR SYSTEM is located), are flying farther apart. Although the universe is getting larger, this does not mean that it has an "edge" like an expanding balloon. This is because the force of GRAVITY in the space between the clusters of galaxies makes anything traveling through it follow a curved path, even though it seems to be straight. Trying to find

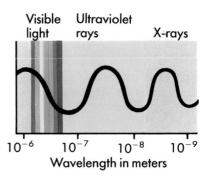

Visible light   Ultraviolet rays   X-rays

10^{-6} 10^{-7} 10^{-8} 10^{-9}
Wavelength in meters

▲ *Ultraviolet rays have shorter wavelengths than visible light and lie beyond the violet end of the spectrum. (10^{-6} meters is 400 thousandths of an inch.)*

Edwin Hubble (1889–1953)
Hubble was an American astronomer whose work provided evidence for the theory that the universe is expanding. In the 1920s he studied hundreds of distant galaxies and, by measuring the red shift in their spectra, showed that they are moving rapidly away from each other. He also classified galaxies into various types.

◄ *The universe is made up of all the galaxies, stars, planets, moons, asteroids, and other bodies scattered through the emptiness of space.*

Edwin Mattison McMillan (1907–)
McMillan is an American physicist who in 1940 made the first element heavier than uranium (element 92). He used neutrons accelerated in a particle accelerator to bombard uranium atoms and produced atoms of element 93, which he called neptunium. For this work, he shared the 1951 Nobel Prize in Physics.

▲ These hands hold a piece of uranium-235, the isotope that is used as a fuel in nuclear reactors. Uranium is one of the densest metals; this small piece weighs 10 pounds and is worth over 200,000 dollars. Before holding the uranium the hands have to be protected with special gloves.

the edge of the universe is like trying to find the "end" of a circle.

The visible universe contains millions of galaxies, collected into clusters and superclusters. These clusters are arranged in a clumpy way instead of being scattered evenly through space. Explaining this "clumping" is a major task in COSMOLOGY.

Astronomers have detected remote galaxies and QUASARS many thousands of millions of light-years away. Even these distant objects are made of the same ATOMS as the ones familiar to us, and obey the laws of physics. We are now used to the idea of the universe being similar everywhere, or "homogeneous," but it was only about a hundred years ago that the law of gravity was proved to operate beyond the Solar System.

Uranium

Uranium is a white METAL. It is an ELEMENT which exists in several varieties, or ISOTOPES, all of which are RADIO-ACTIVE. One of the isotopes, uranium-235, can undergo nuclear fission to release large amounts of ENERGY. It is used in atomic weapons and as the fuel in most types of NUCLEAR REACTORS. Uranium-238 is the fuel in another type of power station, a breeder reactor, which turns it into PLUTONIUM. Uranium occurs in ores such as pitchblende, but is difficult to extract and even more difficult to separate into its isotopes. The mining and extraction of uranium, and its use as a nuclear fuel, create large amounts of radioactive waste products which are difficult to get rid of safely.

See also NUCLEAR PHYSICS; NUCLEAR WASTE.

Glenn Theodore Seaborg (1912–)
Seaborg is an American chemist who specializes in the transuranic elements (the radioactive elements that are heavier than uranium). From 1940, Seaborg and his team produced nine new elements, from plutonium (element 94) to nobelium (element 102). They described the elements' chemical properties. Seaborg shared the 1951 Nobel Prize in Physics.

◀ *Uranus has a faint ring system and 15 moons, 5 large ones and 10 small. Its diameter is four times that of Earth.*

Uranus

Uranus became the first planet to be discovered with a TELESCOPE when William Herschel, observing from Bath, England, found it in 1781. Because it is far away, little was known about it before Voyager 2 sent back closeup observations in 1986, although a dim ring system was detected in 1977. The spacecraft photographed 13 main rings and other very narrow and faint ones.

Five satellites have been known for many years, the largest being Titania 1,000 miles (1,600 km) across and the smallest, Miranda, 300 miles (480 km) across. They are all airless, icy-surfaced bodies with craters where flying fragments crashed into them. The satellite Ariel, has immense valleys, while Miranda is a patchwork of completely different markings. One suggestion is that an old satellite was shattered in a collision, and the fragments drifted together to form Miranda. Voyager discovered 10 new satellites.

Uranus itself is surrounded by a thick ATMOSPHERE of hydrogen, helium, and methane. But unlike the other "cloudy" outer planets it has hardly any cloud markings. The most curious thing about Uranus is the tilt of its axis, which is so tipped over that during its "year" the Sun can shine almost overhead at each pole, and parts of its surface are in continuous day, and then continuous night, for almost 42 of our years.

William Herschel (1738–1822)
Herschel was a German-born British astronomer who in 1781 discovered the planet Uranus using a telescope he had built. He went to Britain as a musician when he was 19, and took up astronomy when he was 36. As well as discovering Uranus, he identified nearly 2,000 nebulae and cataloged 800 double stars. He became astronomer to King George III.

Edward Jenner (1749–1823)
Jenner was a British doctor who in 1796 performed the first successful inoculations against disease. He inoculated people with cowpox (a disease of cattle) to protect them against deadly smallpox. The technique was widely adopted and over the next 100 years deaths from smallpox fell dramatically (from 40 per 10,000 people to 1 per 10,000).

▶ *Vaccination gives active immunity to a disease. It uses killed or weakened germs that have been "grown" in hen's eggs or laboratory animals. Passive immunity results from inoculation with a serum, usually from an animal which has developed immunity to the disease. It can also be given by using a similar, but less dangerous, live germ.*

Vaccination

Vaccination is a medical technique that causes the body to produce substances called ANTIBODIES, which fight DISEASE. Substances which do not naturally belong in the body are called antigens. These cause the IMMUNE SYSTEM to react by producing antibodies which make the antigens harmless. Antigens are carried on the surface of bacteria and viruses.

In vaccination, the antigens which enter the body, through injection or by mouth, are harmless. The vaccine has been treated to weaken the bacteria or virus, and in some cases, dead bacteria or viruses, or even extracts of the antigen substances, will cause the protective antibodies to be produced. Sometimes further vaccinations or boosters are needed to provide continuing protection against infection. To protect against tuberculosis (TB), a similar live but less dangerous bacterium is used to create an infection which causes the body to develop immunity to TB. This is called *inoculation*, and was first used to protect against smallpox, when people were injected with a milder disease called cowpox.

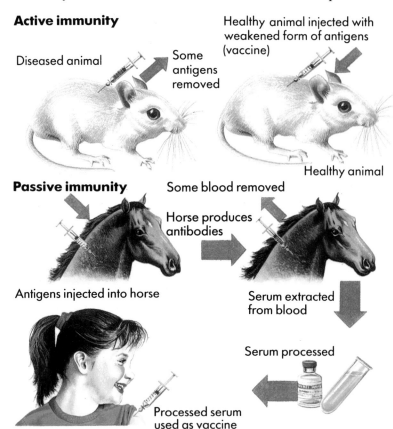

Active immunity

Diseased animal

Some antigens removed

Healthy animal injected with weakened form of antigens (vaccine)

Healthy animal

Passive immunity

Some blood removed

Horse produces antibodies

Antigens injected into horse

Serum extracted from blood

Serum processed

Processed serum used as vaccine

Vacuum

Most of the spaces on Earth which we usually think of as empty are filled with MOLECULES of AIR. A vacuum, on the other hand, is a space which really is empty; a perfect vacuum contains no molecules of any sort. Interstellar space, the open space between the STARS, is almost a perfect vacuum. It is difficult to make a vacuum. It is necessary to pump out all the air from inside a container. However, molecules of air can leak in through very tiny

The best vacuums so far produced measure approximately 0.0000000001 pascal (one pascal equals a pressure of about 0.00015 pound per square inch). Even at this very low pressure, 1 cubic inch (16 cc) of gas contains over 500,000 molecules. A cc of normal air contains about 400 billion molecules.

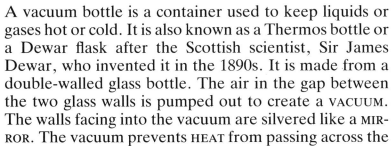

holes in the container and molecules on the surface of the container evaporate into the empty space. The container must also be strong enough to withstand the inward PRESSURE of the air outside. Something which is nearly a vacuum is called a *partial vacuum*. A vacuum is useful as thermal INSULATION because it prevents heat flow by CONVECTION. Foods such as coffee which become stale when exposed to air, are packed in a "vacuum pack" from which the air has been removed.
See also EVAPORATION; MAGDEBURG SPHERES.

◀ Any container with a lower pressure on the inside than on the outside must be very strong. If a little water is boiled in a metal can, the water produces steam which expands. If the can is taken off the heat and the cap screwed on, the steam will cool and condense lowering the pressure inside the can, forming a partial vacuum. After a short time, the air pressure will crush the can inward.

▼ An upright vacuum cleaner has an electric motor that sucks air from the bottom of the dust bag. This leaves a partial vacuum which causes dust to be pushed up by the outside air pressure into the bag.

Vacuum bottle

A vacuum bottle is a container used to keep liquids or gases hot or cold. It is also known as a Thermos bottle or a Dewar flask after the Scottish scientist, Sir James Dewar, who invented it in the 1890s. It is made from a double-walled glass bottle. The air in the gap between the two glass walls is pumped out to create a VACUUM. The walls facing into the vacuum are silvered like a MIRROR. The vacuum prevents HEAT from passing across the

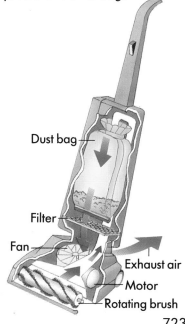

Dust bag

Filter

Fan

Exhaust air

Motor

Rotating brush

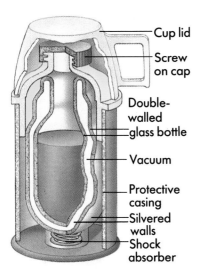

Sir James Dewar (1842–1923)
Dewar was a British chemist and physicist who in about 1892 invented the vacuum bottle, also called a Dewar flask. It is sometimes known by its trade name, Thermos bottle. Dewar used the bottle in experiments with liquid oxygen, hydrogen, and other gases at very low temperatures. In 1891, with Frederick Abel, he developed cordite, a smokeless propellant explosive for cartridges and shells.

▲ *A vacuum bottle keeps hot liquids hot or cold liquids cold by preventing the transfer of heat between the contents and the outside. The vacuum prevents heat flow by convection, and silvering on the bottle's walls prevents heat flow by radiation.*

The American inventor Thomas Edison produced the first vacuum tube, but he did not realize its importance. Early in the 1880s, Edison sealed an extra electrode into a light bulb. He noticed that a current flowed from the bulb's filament to this electrode if it was positively charged. Edison had made a diode vacuum tube, but he could see no use for his invention.

▶ *In a diode tube, electrons travel from the heated cathode (negative electrode) to the anode (positive electrode). A triode has a similar arrangement of electrodes but in addition has a control grid. This is between the cathode and anode, and its voltage is adjusted to control the flow of electrons.*

gap by contact with air molecules. This transfer of heat is called CONVECTION. The silvering reflects heat, preventing it from crossing the gap by RADIATION. In 1925 a vacuum bottle enclosed in a case for protection first went on sale to the public for carrying hot or cold drinks.

Vacuum tube

A vacuum tube is a device that works by the action of ELECTRONS traveling through a gas or a VACUUM. Inside the tube's glass body, electrons flow from an electrically-heated electrode (the cathode) through the gas or vacuum to a second electrode, (the anode). There may be other electrodes between the cathode and anode which control the flow of electrons.

There are different types of vacuum tubes. The first,

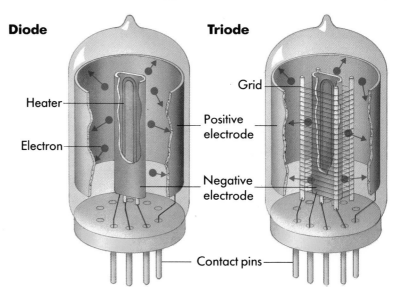

Diode

Triode

Heater

Electron

Grid

Positive electrode

Negative electrode

Contact pins

the diode, was invented in 1904. Electrons travel through it in one direction only, enabling it to convert alternating current to direct current. The triode, invented in 1910, is used to amplify electrical signals. Other types of tubes include the tetrode and pentode. Vacuum tubes have now been largely replaced by the semiconductor DIODE, TRANSISTOR, and INTEGRATED CIRCUIT.

Valency

Valency is the combining power of a chemical ELEMENT. It tells us how many chemical BONDS an element can form when it combines with other elements in COMPOUNDS. These bonds involve ELECTRONS, and so the valency is the number of electrons an element can give, take, or share in forming bonds. Some elements always have the same valency. For hydrogen it is always one, for oxygen it is two, and for carbon it is four. Other elements have more than one valency. Iron, for example, can combine to form compounds in two ways and so has a valency of two in some of its compounds, and in other compounds its valency is three.

▲ Special vacuum tubes are used to generate radio waves. This large tube was the key component in an early short-wave radio transmitter.

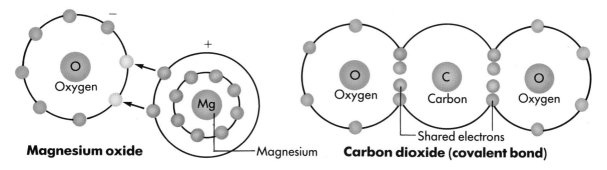

Magnesium oxide

Carbon dioxide (covalent bond)

Van Allen belts

Van Allen belts are two "shells" of atomic particles sent out by the SUN, trapped in space around the EARTH by its magnetic field. They consist of ELECTRONS and PROTONS, and the inner one is about 2,000 miles (3,000 km) above the Earth, the outer one is about 10,000 miles (16,000 km) away.

The Van Allen belts are denser places in the Earth's magnetosphere. The magnetosphere is a huge volume of space, pushed into a comet shape by the SOLAR WIND, extending about 60,000 miles (100,000 km) toward the Sun and about a million miles away from it.

These two magnetic fields are like a vast generator

▲ Magnesium and oxygen both have a valency of two. The left-hand diagram shows how magnesium can give its two outer electrons to fill oxygen's outer shell (to give it eight electrons), forming the compound magnesium oxide. Carbon has four outer electrons and a valency of four. The right-hand diagram shows how one atom of carbon can combine with two oxygen atoms to form carbon dioxide.

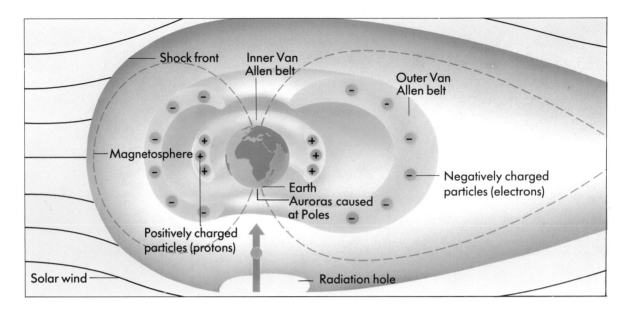

Shock front

Inner Van Allen belt

Outer Van Allen belt

Magnetosphere

Negatively charged particles (electrons)

Earth
Auroras caused at Poles

Positively charged particles (protons)

Solar wind

Radiation hole

▲ *The Van Allen radiation belts around the Earth are part of the magnetosphere. The belts are distorted by the solar wind so that they are much closer to the surface of the Earth on the side of the Earth that faces the Sun.*

creating ELECTRICITY. The ENERGY is carried down by particles into the Earth's atmosphere, causing the glows known as AURORAS. These two belts were discovered in 1958 by the American physicist James Van Allen.

Van de Graaff generator

A Van de Graaff generator is a machine used to produce very high voltages. It was invented in the 1930s by the American physicist, Robert Jemison Van de Graaff. It consists of a hollow metal hemisphere or dome supported on top of an insulated pillar. A belt made from an electrical INSULATOR is wound around two rollers, one at the top of the pillar inside the dome and one at the bot-

Scientists planning the first Apollo trips to the Moon were worried about the effects of the radiation in the Van Allen belts on the astronauts. It turned out that there was less danger than had been feared. The thickness of the spacecraft's outer layer was enough to protect the astronauts.

▶ *At a science demonstration, a high-voltage charge of static electricity from a Van de Graaff generator makes this girl's hair stand on end. Each hair tries to push away from the next one because the like charges repel and the hairs all have the same static charge.*

tom. The belt is driven around the rollers. As the belt travels past a row of metal points next to the bottom roller, it acquires a positive charge. The belt carries the charge up inside the dome where it is transferred to the dome and moves to the dome's outer surface. The charge continues to build up on the dome, which may reach an electric potential of up to 13 million volts. *See also* STATIC ELECTRICITY.

Vapor

A vapor is a GAS that can exist at the same TEMPERATURE as the LIQUID or SOLID from which it comes. Unlike a gas above a certain temperature, a vapor can be liquefied by PRESSURE alone without being cooled.

After it has been raining and the Sun comes out, any puddles soon dry up. This is because when a liquid such as rainwater evaporates, ATOMS or MOLECULES leave its surface and form a vapor. When a liquid is heated, it changes to a vapor more rapidly than when the surroundings are cold. For example when water boils, it changes to a vapor, in this case STEAM, very quickly. If a vapor is cooled, it changes back into a liquid. In a steamy room, water vapor (steam) condenses on the window to form water. Sometimes when the temperature drops at the end of the day, water vapor in the air condenses as droplets of water that form mist or fog.

If a vapor is compressed, it changes back into a liquid. This cycle of changes is used in REFRIGERATION. A vapor is compressed to make a liquid, and then the

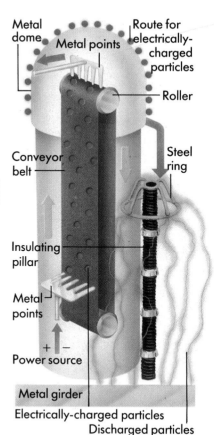

▲ *A Van de Graaff generator uses a conveyor belt to carry electric charge and store it on a metal dome. The charge is picked up from a metal comb connected to a high-voltage electricity supply. A large enough charge of discharged particles (at millions of volts) can jump from the steel ring, ionizing the surrounding air and flashing to the ground like artificial lightning.*

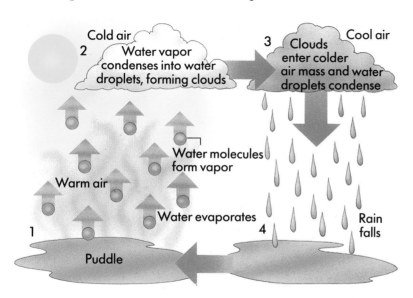

◄ *1. Puddles dry up in the Sun as the water in them is changed to vapor. 2. High in the sky, the vapor forms clouds of water droplets 3. These droplets combine to form drops of rain when the cloud is cooled 4. The rain falls and the water that lies on the ground forms puddles.*

liquid is allowed to evaporate back into a vapor. This stage requires HEAT and the heat is taken from the inside of the refrigerator, thereby keeping the contents cool. *See also* CONDENSATION; EVAPORATION.

Variable stars

Most stars shine with a steady light, but some vary in brightness over periods from hours to years. A few of these "variable" stars do not actually change in light output at all, but appear to do so because they are twin or BINARY STARS. As they orbit each other, the light from one is blocked out for a time, and they are known as eclipsing binaries. True variables are usually unstable single stars that swell out and shrink, or binary stars where gas passes from one to the other and suddenly flares up. The unstable stars usually repeat this cycle of

▲ *Clouds of vapor form around a horse's nostrils. In the cold air, water vapor in the animal's breath condenses to form minute droplets of water.*

▶ *Variable stars change in brightness. Sometimes this is not because the star flares up or dims. For example, a binary star consists of two stars orbiting each other. It appears bright when both stars are visible and less bright when one is hidden behind the other.*

▼ *The brightness of a variable star changes as the star swells and shrinks. Many of these stars pulsate regularly at a rate of a few hours or days.*

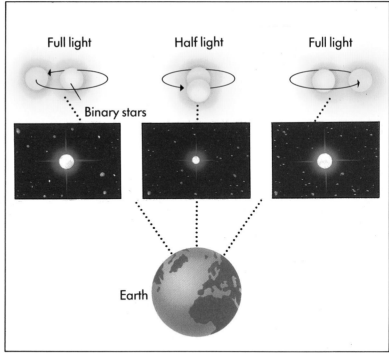

Full light   Half light   Full light

Binary stars

Earth

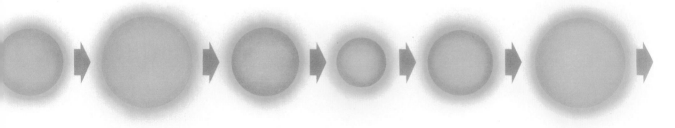

brightening and fading at regular intervals, while the explosive binaries are unpredictable. Other types of variables include flare stars (single stars that have brilliant surges of light), and the rare stars that are usually bright, but become dim as clouds form around them.

Velocity

Velocity is the rate at which an object's position changes. Velocity involves two pieces of information: the first is the speed at which the object is moving, and the second is the direction in which it is moving. If either of these two things changes, then the velocity changes, so two objects traveling with the same speed in different directions have different velocities. It is important not to confuse speed and velocity: speed refers to how fast an object is moving while velocity refers not only to the object's speed but to the direction it is moving in as well. The rate of change of the velocity is called the ACCELERATION, and the rate of change of position of an object is called speed. Velocity and acceleration are important in MECHANICS, the study of moving things.

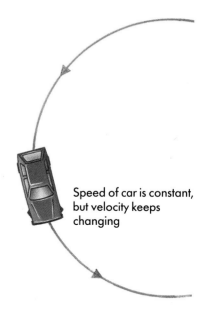

Speed of car is constant, but velocity keeps changing

▲ *Speed is the rate of change of position — how far something goes in a given time. Velocity is the speed in a particular direction. So a car driving in a circle can have a constant speed, but its velocity keeps on changing because the car keeps pointing in a different direction.*

◄ *A camera freezes the action as a bullet traveling at a velocity of 1,480 feet per second (450 m/s) (nearly one and a half times faster than sound travels) hits a raw egg.*

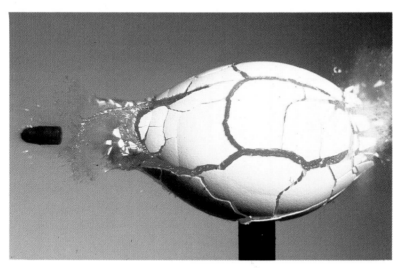

Velocity is measured in units such as miles per hour or meters per second (m/s). The theory of RELATIVITY tells us that the largest possible velocity is the velocity of light, which is about 186,000 miles (300 million meters) per second.
See also CENTRIFUGAL FORCE; MOVEMENT AND MOTION.

Vein *See* Circulation

Stopping Distances
The faster vehicles are traveling, the greater the distance of road they need to stop. An ordinary car traveling at 30 mph (50 km/h) needs about 75 feet (23 m) to come to a stop, whereas a car traveling at 50 mph (80 km/h) needs 174 feet (53 m). This is because of the momentum of the vehicle which combines its velocity and its mass. A large truck needs more room to stop in than a car.

VENUS FACTS
Diameter
7,700 miles (12,104 km)
Distance from Sun
67,000,000 miles
(108,000,000 km)
Year length 225 days
Day length 117 Earth days
Mass 0.82 Earths
Density 0.89 Earth
Surface temperature
896°F (480°C) (maximum)
Atmosphere mainly carbon
dioxide gas.

▶ The hot surface of Venus is hidden behind the dense clouds of its thick, poisonous atmosphere.

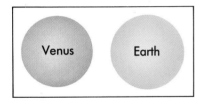

▲ Venus is about the same size as Earth. Unusually, Venus takes longer to spin on its axis (243 days) than it takes the planet to orbit the Sun (225 days).

▼ The space probe Magellan has sent back to Earth the best pictures yet of Venus. The planet is possibly the most unpleasant place in the Solar System.

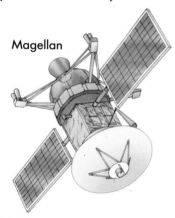

Magellan

Venus

Venus is a PLANET that orbits the SUN between the EARTH and MERCURY, and is almost exactly the same size as the Earth. But it is very different from our planet. The surface of Venus is the hottest place in the SOLAR SYSTEM, with a temperature reaching 896°F (480°C). It is a rocky windswept planet with an "atmosphere" that would feel thicker than ocean water at a depth of several hundred feet. This atmosphere contains carbon dioxide, sulfuric acid and other poisonous compounds, and lightning flickers between the clouds.

Sunlight falls on the rocky surface that warms up and gives out heat RADIATION. The carbon dioxide surrounding Venus lets in enough sunlight to heat the ground, but does not let out the heat radiated from the ground. The heat is trapped, releasing more carbon dioxide from the rocks and making the heat blanket even more efficient. This "runaway GREENHOUSE EFFECT" has turned Venus into an oven.

The invisible surface has been mapped by RADAR from Earth and from SPACE PROBES. Mountain peaks up to 7 miles (12km) high have been charted. Some features look like Earth-type VOLCANOES. From measurements of the sulfur dioxide gas in Venus's atmosphere, it appears that one or more of the volcanoes may still be active, throwing out sulfur dioxide when it erupts.

Very high frequency (VHF)

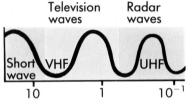

Very high frequency (VHF) is the name given to RADIO waves whose FREQUENCY is higher than the frequency of other radio waves but not as high as ULTRAHIGH FREQUENCY waves (UHF). VHF waves have frequencies of around 100 MHz (one hundred million cycles per second), while other radio waves have frequencies of up to only a few hundred kHz (a few hundred thousand hertz). The higher frequency of VHF means that the signal can carry much more information than ordinary radio waves. The disadvantage of VHF signals,

▲ VHF radio waves, which lie between short waves and radar waves in the electromagnetic spectrum, are mainly used for television and high-quality radio broadcasting.

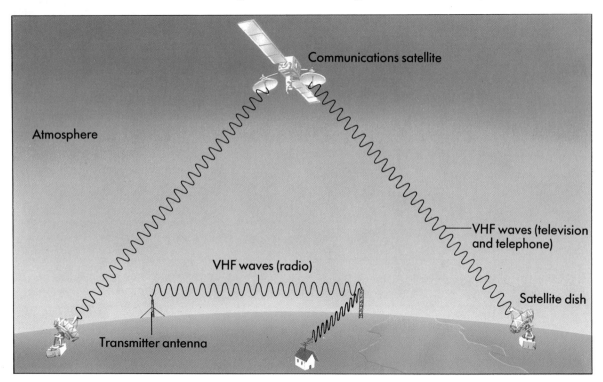

▲ VHF radio waves can be used for communication only between places that are within sight of each other. Even with a very tall mast for the transmitting antenna an effective range is only about 50 miles (80 km) overland. But communications satellites allow much greater ranges, and VHF signals to and from a satellite can span an ocean or a whole continent.

however, is that they are not diffracted very easily over hills and, unlike lower-frequency radio waves, they are not reflected from the IONOSPHERE. This means that they are not very effective in transmitting radio signals over very long distances or in mountainous areas.

VHF radio signals are usually different from others because the frequency, rather than the amplitude, of the radio wave is changed when the sound signal is added to the carrier wave. This is called frequency modulation (FM) rather than amplitude modulation (AM).

Vesalius, Andreas *See* Muscles

VETERINARY MEDICINE

Veterinary medicine is concerned with the health and treatment of animals. Experiments and surgery on animals have been used for centuries to train doctors, but now veterinary medicine is a highly specialized science in its own right. The training is similar to that for medical doctors, but is in some ways more complicated, because of the many different animals which must be studied. The veterinarian must be highly skilled at making a diagnosis because, unlike humans, animals cannot help the diagnosis by describing how they feel.

Veterinary medicine can be divided into two groups. Small animal veterinary medicine is concerned with the health and treatment of domestic animals such as cats, dogs, and other small pets. A large animal veterinary practice looks after farm livestock and horses, and is generally concerned with preventing illness in these animals, as much as treating them once they are sick. Veterinarians routinely treat farm livestock to remove worms and other parasites which slow their growth or reduce milk production. Vaccines are available to immunize domestic pets and farm livestock against common diseases.

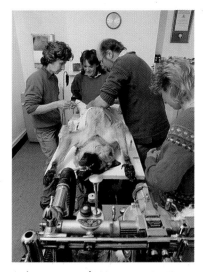

▲ In towns and cities, veterinarians see mainly domestic animals kept as pets. They treat animals that are ill or injured and also immunize them against common diseases and administer other preventative care. Here a dog is undergoing surgery.

◄ In agricultural communities, veterinarians treat farm animals to keep them healthy and prevent the outbreak of diseases. Herds of cattle or other groups of animals are at danger from epidemics of animal diseases because the disease can spread very quickly. Whole herds of animals could die and infect the animals belonging to other farmers nearby. On this farm, the cattle are being given an injection of a drug to combat internal parasites.

Some Common Animal Diseases

Animal diseases need to be treated before the disease can spread to other animals. Many animal diseases can be transmitted to humans.
Brucellosis an infectious disease of cattle, goats, and pigs which causes fever.
Psittacosis a viral disease of parrots and other birds that is similar to pneumonia.
Rabies a very infectious viral disease which affects the nervous system and in dogs, causes foaming at the mouth.
Tuberculosis an infectious disease which mostly affects the lungs. Tuberculosis in cattle can be passed to humans.

Some exotic animals such as gorillas, lions, and tigers, are treated by veterinarians. All of these animals need dental care in captivity. Special techniques are used to help breed some endangered species that are dying out in the wild. Veterinarians are employed by zoos to keep rare animals healthy.

See also AGRICULTURE; BIOLOGY; BREEDING; DISEASE; ENDANGERED SPECIES; PARASITE; PATHOLOGY; VACCINATION; ZOOLOGY.

Video camera

A video camera is used to convert an image into an electrical signal that can form a picture on a TELEVISION screen or be recorded on video TAPE.

Light enters the camera through a LENS. This bends the light rays together so that they form a sharp image on a light-sensitive plate called a target. The target is normally charged up to about 30 volts. When light falls on it, the voltage leaks away. A brightly lit part of the target may fall to zero volts. The pickup tube produces an ELECTRON beam that scans across the target. It restores each part of the target to its fully charged state. The bright parts of the target require greater charging than the darker parts. This charging current forms the video signal from the camera.

Although many cameras used in television studios still have pickup tubes, most home video cameras and camcorders (a camcorder is a combined camera and recorder) use a different light sensor called a charge coupled device or CCD. This SEMICONDUCTOR device is much smaller than a pickup tube, is less fragile than the glass tube and it is not damaged by exposure to very bright light as the pickup tube can be.

See also VIDEO RECORDER.

All cameras have to be held steady so that the pictures produced will be clear. Originally, movie cameras had to run on rails similar to those used by trains to keep them steady. Steadicam is a system that allows a video camera operator to move around freely without the picture becoming wobbly and unsteady. It has a harness for the camera operator and a system of springs and levers to absorb any sudden movements. It works somewhat like the suspension of a car in flattening out bumps.

Camcorder

▶ *A modern amateur video camera, called a camcorder, records pictures and sound on a small cassette of videotape. The tape can be played back through an ordinary television using a video recorder.*

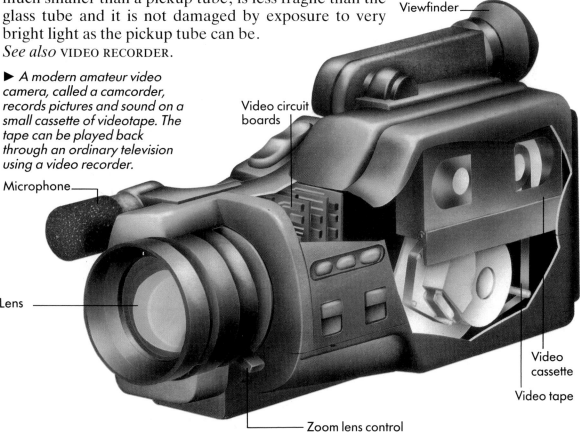

Viewfinder

Video circuit boards

Microphone

Lens

Video cassette

Video tape

Zoom lens control

Videocassette recorder

A videocassette recorder is a machine used to store moving pictures on magnetic TAPE. It receives signals through a cable connected to the TELEVISION antenna. As in an audio CASSETTE RECORDER, the tape is held against a spinning metal drum containing the recording heads. The drum is set at an angle to the tape. Each revolution of the drum records a single television picture across the width of the tape. To record, an erase head removes any existing magnetic pattern from the tape and a video head records new picture signals as a diagonal pattern on the magnetic tape. Sound signals are recorded along one edge of the tape by the audio head.

▲ Modern home videocassette recorders often have a wide variety of features to control both recording and playback. Many now have remote control devices that send infrared signals to the recorder to operate these features.

The first video recorder was developed in 1956 by the U.S. Ampex Corporation. It recorded television pictures a line at a time across the width of 50mm (2-inch) wide magnetic tape. The first video recorder for home use was developed by the European Philips company in 1972. The most popular home video system or format is now VHS, the Video Home System developed by JVC in Japan in the mid 1970s.

How a Videocassette Recorder works

A VCR stores signals for sound and pictures, received by the television antenna, on separate tracks on the videotape. An audio head records the sound on a narrow track, and an angled video head records the pictures on a zig-zag track that occupies most of the rest of the tape. There is also a narrow control track.

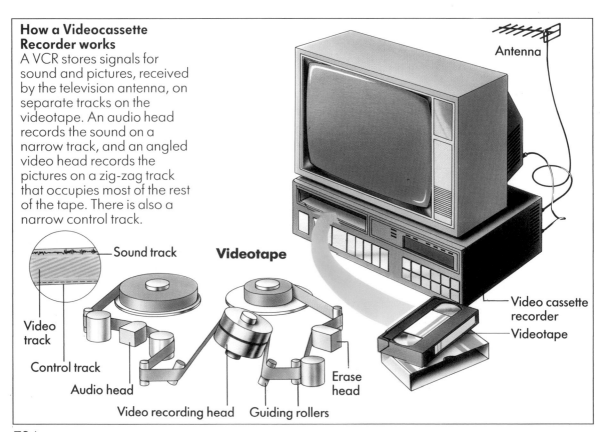

Sound track

Videotape

Video track

Control track

Audio head

Video recording head

Guiding rollers

Erase head

Antenna

Video cassette recorder

Videotape

VIRUSES AND VIRAL DISEASES ⊞

Viruses are tiny organisms which nearly always produce diseases in animals and plants. All viruses are parasites which can live only in other life forms. Technically, they are not living creatures at all, because they can reproduce and carry out the normal processes of life only when they are inside a cell, and forming a part of the cell's structure. Viruses invade cells and take over the genetic material (DNA and RNA), changing its function so that the whole cell becomes a "factory" producing viruses. Eventually the cell bursts and dies, releasing the new viruses to spread.

Because the function of the cell is affected, infection with viruses nearly always causes disease. The body's usual defenses cannot easily fight the virus, because once the virus is inside the cell, the body's immune system is unable to recognize the invader. Antibodies can attack the virus only when it bursts out of the cell ready to infect other cells. Drugs such as antibiotics do not work against viruses, and the immune system must be relied upon to fight the infection. The HIV virus, which can cause AIDS, is particularly dangerous because it infects and kills the cells of the immune system which normally fight diseases. Virus particles, or virions, are very tiny. Viral diseases are usually spread by viruses carried in water droplets in the air, which are inhaled into the lungs. Colds and influenza are common infections caused by viruses.

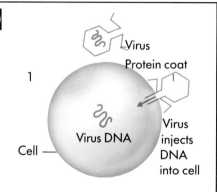
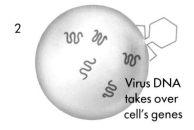

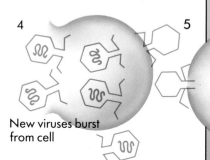

Cell — Virus DNA
Virus
Protein coat
Virus injects DNA into cell

1

2 Virus DNA takes over cell's genes

3 New viruses produced

4   5
New viruses burst from cell

▲ *1. A virus consists of a strand of genetic material (DNA or RNA) inside a protein coat. It infects a cell by injecting its DNA into the cell 2. The viral DNA takes over the cell and 3. makes the cell produce more viruses 4. Eventually the infected cell bursts, releasing the new viruses that go on to attack more cells 5.*

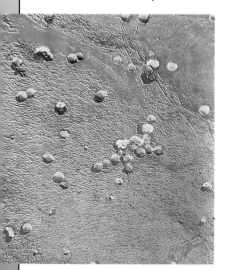

▲ *A false-color picture taken with an electron microscope shows particles of the virus adenovirus (yellow), similar to the type that cause the common cold. The tiny organism is magnified here 25,000 times.*

Viral Diseases

Diseases caused by viruses include some of the most dangerous and most annoying of all illnesses. Some of them (but by no means all) can be prevented by vaccination, but treatment is usually limited to relieving the symptoms. Antibiotics, effective against most bacterial diseases, are useless against viruses. Viral diseases include:

AIDS (acquired immune
    deficiency syndrome)
Chicken pox
Common cold
Influenza
Measles
Mumps
Polio
Rabies
Rubella (German measles)

See also AIDS; ANTIBIOTICS; ANTIBODIES AND ANTIGENS; CELL; DISEASE; IMMUNE SYSTEM; INFECTION; PARASITE; VACCINATION.

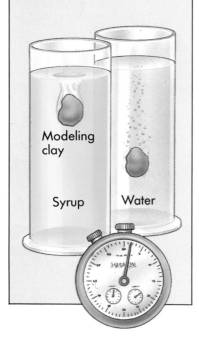

Modeling clay

Syrup   Water

Viscosity

Viscosity describes the ability of FLUIDS (GASES or LIQUIDS) to flow. The property of flowing is called the fluidity, resistance to flow is the viscosity. It is a type of FRICTION force. If an object is moved through a fluid, the fluid next to the object is carried along with it. The nearby fluid is therefore moving relative to the fluid farther away from the object and the resistance which is produced pulls the object back. This backward force from the viscosity can be reduced by STREAMLINING. Different fluids have different viscosities; a gas such as air has a very low viscosity, since the MOLECULES in it do not pull on each other very much. Liquids lose some of their viscosity as they are heated because their molecules do not interact as much as they grow hotter. However, hot gases have a higher viscosity than cold gases.

Visual display unit (VDU)

A visual display unit or VDU is part of a COMPUTER. It shows visual information such as text and COMPUTER GRAPHICS on a screen. The most common type of VDU is the CATHODE-RAY TUBE or CRT. A CRT works like a TELEVISION screen. It builds up the picture from hundreds of lines of glowing phosphor dots. It may be monochrome (single-color) or color. Alternatives to the CRT include the plasma panel, LIQUID CRYSTAL DISPLAY (LCD), and electroluminescent display. They use glowing NEON gas, LIQUID CRYSTALS, and glowing phosphors respectively to form images. These flat panel displays are more compact and less fragile than the glass CRT.

▶ *A visual display unit, or VDU, connected to a computer can show alphanumeric characters (letters and numbers) so can be used with word processing software to display text. VDUs can also be used with computer graphics programs to display graphs and charts.*

Vitamins

Vitamins are substances that our bodies need to help the many CHEMICAL REACTIONS which take place inside the CELLS. Vitamins cannot be made inside the body (except some vitamin D which can be made in the skin), so they must be obtained from the food we eat. There are several types of vitamins, which are found in a very wide range of foods. Some vitamins dissolve in body fat and can be stored in this way, so they are needed only in very small amounts in our food. Others such as vitamin C dissolve in water, and are flushed out in our urine, so we need to constantly supplement the amounts in our body. Vitamins and MINERALS are important nutrients which help to build cells.

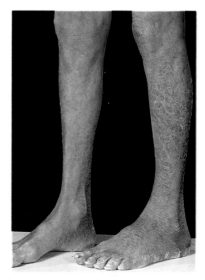

▲ This person is suffering from pellagra. The disorder results from a lack of one type of vitamin B in the diet and causes broken skin and weakness in the muscles. The type of vitamin B missing is needed by the body to obtain energy from glucose. Without it the tissues of the body lose a lot of energy.

Vitamin	Usual Sources	Action in Body
Vitamin A	Liver, fish oils, dairy products, fruit, and vegetables	Needed for healthy eyes, skin, and tissues
Vitamin B (several types)	Meat, dairy products, whole grains (as in wholemeal flour and bread), vegetables	Used by cells in the release of energy, and in red blood cell production
Vitamin C (ascorbic acid)	Oranges, lemons, many other fruits, and vegetables	Needed for healthy bones and teeth, and for tissue repair
Vitamin D	Oily fish, dairy products, and eggs. Some vitamin D is made in the skin by sunlight.	Needed for bone growth
Vitamin E	Brown flour, wheat-germ, liver, green vegetables	In humans no proved function
Vitamin K	Leafy vegetables. Also made in the intestines by harmless bacteria	Helps with blood clotting

In Western countries, the type and amounts of food available mean that people are rarely deficient in vitamins. Where famine and malnutrition are common, vitamin deficiency can be serious, particularly in children. Deficiencies of vitamin D cause rickets, a disease in which the bones do not harden properly, so the legs become deformed. This often affects children where the diet consists mainly of rice, even though some vitamin D is made when sunlight falls on the skin. Vitamin supplements are not necessary if a balanced diet is eaten.

▲ A properly balanced diet will contain all the vitamins that a person needs. It should include milk and dairy products, bread, meat and fish or legumes, and plenty of fresh fruit and vegetables.

► *An erupting volcano can produce thousands of tons of lava. Red-hot lava can have a temperature of over 1,800°F.*

The world's most devastating volcanic eruption took place at Tambora, Indonesia in 1815 when 12,000 people were killed. The volcano threw out about 36 cubic miles (150 cubic km) of ash and dust. Later in the 19th century when Krakatau, also in Indonesia, exploded, more than 35,000 people were drowned by a giant ocean wave (tsunami).

Volcano Facts
There are about 850 active volcanoes in the world, of which 75 percent are part of the "Ring of Fire." The word "volcano" comes from the Latin name *Volcanus* for the ancient god of fire. Near Sicily, Italy, there is an island called Vulcano with an active volcano on it.

The best-documented volcanic eruption was that of Mount St. Helens in the state of Washington in 1980. For several weeks before the eruption the volcano's activity was monitored by scientists. Despite all this care 60 people died, one of whom was one of the observing scientists. He was too close because the eruption was more powerful than expected. The volcano has erupted several times.

► *Most volcanoes are found along or close to the edges of the plates that make up the Earth's crust. The plates float on the Earth's red-hot core. Their movements cause the flow of hot material to the surface that leads to volcanic eruptions.*

Volcanoes

Volcanoes are the various vents or cracks in the crust of the EARTH through which molten rock or LAVA, gas, steam, ash, and even solid ROCK material may be forced out to the surface. The shape of a volcano depends largely on the type of material forced out.

Volcanic eruptions take place in those parts of the Earth's crust where there is a large flow of heat from within the mantle. This is usually along the margins of plates that carry the land and sea. Some volcanoes, such as those which make up the Hawaiian islands, occur within a plate itself and these tend to be less violent than

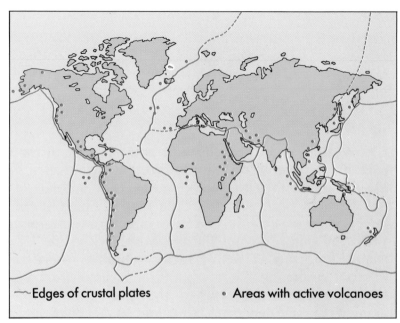

— Edges of crustal plates   • Areas with active volcanoes

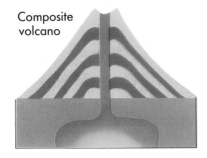

Composite volcano

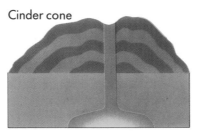

Cinder cone

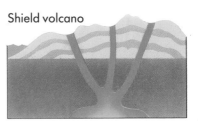

Shield volcano

▲ *There are three main types of volcano which each have distinctive cones. A composite volcano erupts regularly, spilling* | *out lava and cinders that flow down the sides and cool to form a cone-shaped mountain. A cinder volcano throws out ash* | *and builds a flatter cone. A shield volcano is flatter still and has several openings where lava wells up to the surface.*

those which occur at plate margins. There are so many volcanoes around the boundary of the Pacific plate that it is known as the "Pacific ring of fire."

Volcanoes, such as those of the Hawaiian islands, force out large amounts of thin lava so that the volcanic cone is low and spreads out to cover a wide area. Layer after layer of lava, ash, and debris builds up gradually to form the elegantly shaped cone.

In some volcanoes, the vent becomes blocked between eruptions by a plug of rock. Slowly, the pressure under the plug builds up and the volcano erupts with such force and speed that no one has any time to escape. For example, the ancient city of Pompeii in southwest Italy was buried by an eruption of Vesuvius in A.D. 79.

Volt

The volt is the SI UNIT that measures voltage. Voltage is also known as electromotive force (e.m.f.) or "potential difference." This is the difference in the ENERGY of an electric charge at two different points. Work must be done to push an electric current through a wire. To do this work there must be a voltage — a difference in potential — between one end of the wire and the other. An ordinary flashlight battery produces 1½ volts. Most household appliances run on 110 volts. One volt of potential difference across a RESISTANCE of one ohm produces a current of one AMPERE.

Voltages are measured using a voltmeter; these can work by using the voltage to be measured to send an electric current through a resistance. The magnetic field of this current then moves the needle on the voltmeter's scale to show how many volts are flowing. More accurate

SEE FOR YOURSELF
The molten rock called magma moves through the Earth's crust under pressure. You can produce a similar effect if you roll up a nearly-finished tube of toothpaste. The pressure squeezes the paste toward the cap. Make a small hole near the cap and keep squeezing, toothpaste will ooze out of the hole like lava from a volcano.

▶ *The voltage between two points in a circuit is measured using a voltmeter. The voltmeter has a high internal resistance. It works by using the magnetic effect of the small current flowing through it to produce movement which makes a needle move around a scale. The size of the current affects the amount the needle moves against the scale and this indicates the size of voltage.*

The discovery of vulcanization in 1838 was a turning point in the rubber industry. Before then, rubber products were of little use because they stiffened in winter and became soft and sticky in summer. Then, one day, Charles Goodyear accidentally dropped a rubber sulfur mixture he was experimenting with onto a hot stove. Instead of melting, the rubber became firm and strong.

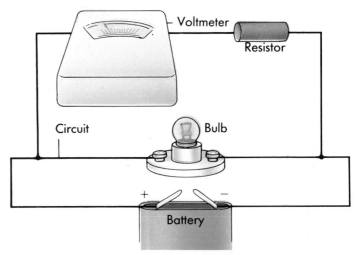

DIGITAL voltmeters are often used today. The volt is named after the Italian scientist Alessandro Volta. *See also* ELECTRICITY; GALVANOMETER.

Volta, Alessandro *See* Electricity

Volume *See* Measurement

Vulcanizing

Vulcanizing is a process for hardening rubber. The RUB-BER extracted from the tree is sticky and plastic. It is vulcanized by heating with SULFUR or sulfur compounds. The MOLECULES in unvulcanized rubber have a long zigzag shape. They straighten when the rubber is stretched and break fairly easily. Vulcanizing causes the long molecules to form chemical BONDS that join them side to side. This makes the rubber tougher and stronger. It still stretches when pulled, but snaps back to its former shape when the force is removed. *See also* ELASTICITY.

▼ *Unvulcanized rubber is soft and easily broken. It is used in erasers for removing pencil marks. Heating rubber with sulfur causes chemical bonds to form between the rubber's long hydrocarbon molecules. The resulting vulcanized rubber is very much harder and stronger, and is used for making vehicle tires.*

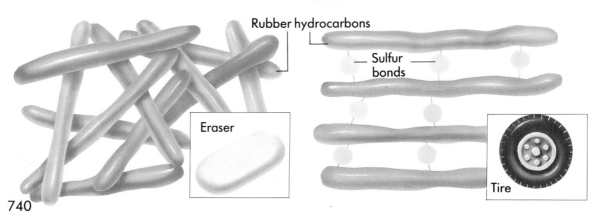

Wankel engine

The Wankel engine is a type of INTERNAL-COMBUSTION ENGINE. It was invented by the German engineer, Felix Wankel, in the 1950s. In an ordinary engine, the up and down motion of the pistons has to be converted into a rotary motion to drive the wheels. The link between the engine and wheels could be simplified if the pistons themselves rotated. In the Wankel engine, a triangular piston rotates inside a chamber shaped like an eight. As it rotates, FUEL and air are sucked in through a valve, compressed, and ignited by an electrical spark. The burning gases expand and drive the piston around.

The first car powered by a Wankel engine was the NSU Wankel Spyder. Despite the small size of the engine (500cc), the car had a top speed of 94 mph (152 km/h). The early engines suffered from several problems. The seals between the rotating piston and the chamber wore down, allowing gases to leak from one side of the piston to the others. It used fuel more quickly than other engines and produced high levels of exhaust.

▼ As in most internal-combustion engines, the Wankel engine works using a cycle of four stages: drawing in fuel and air (intake), compressing the fuel/air mixture (compression), igniting the mixture to generate power (power), and getting rid of the burned gases (exhaust). It does this with a single rotating piston and two spark plugs.

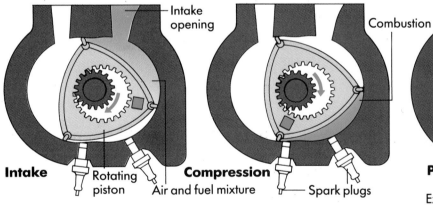

Intake — Intake opening, Rotating piston, Air and fuel mixture, **Compression** — Spark plugs, Combustion, **Power** — Ignition

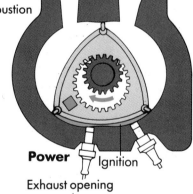

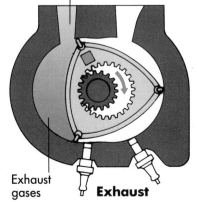

Exhaust opening, Exhaust gases, **Exhaust**

Waste disposal

Waste disposal refers to the methods people use to get rid of materials, often called refuse, which they no longer need. Humans have become a problem for the ENVIRONMENT because of their rapidly increasing population. Human waste or sewage, for example, needs treatment to make it harmless. Sewage is sometimes disposed of into the sea. This can lead to overloading of the natural processes of decay which can spread disease or cause rapid growths of possibly harmful algae.

People produce huge quantities of waste. Containers,

Recycling plant

Solid waste from water works used as fertilizer

Sewer

Water from drains

▲ *Most wastes have to be treated to make them safe before they are released into the environment. An exception is rainwater that runs off the surface of the land, and can be piped into a river. Water waste from our homes has to be treated at a sewage plant before it can be released.*

▲ *At a well-managed landfill site, waste is compacted together and then sealed off by being covered with soil. It is important that the waste is covered to prevent smells and to stop animals such as rats from living in it.*

such as bottles and cans, which once filled garbage cans, can now be recycled. Much of our waste is buried and these sites are then used for construction. Other waste is burned in incinerators, usually in large cities. The by-products of many industries can be very poisonous and, in recent years, strict controls have been introduced to prevent companies from releasing untreated waste into rivers, seas, or the atmosphere. The NUCLEAR WASTE from nuclear power stations produces separate problems.

Water

More than two-thirds of the human body is made of water, and some animals, such as jellyfish, are almost 100 percent water. The very first forms of life which appeared on EARTH evolved in a watery ENVIRONMENT and this transparent LIQUID is vital to every living thing on our planet. *See* pages 744 and 745.

Water pollution

Water in rivers, lakes, and streams almost always contains dissolved chemicals or carries debris suspended in it. Water is described as polluted if the amounts or kinds of substances contained in it are likely to cause harm to humans, other animals, plants, or the ENVIRONMENT.

Rivers and seas have traditionally been used for WASTE DISPOSAL. Fast-flowing rivers are able to transport sewage and other waste away to the oceans where the natural processes of decay can usually cope with the waste. But, in slower-flowing waters or where more

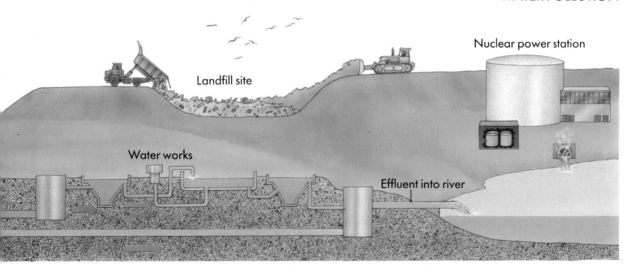

▲ Although many materials, such as paper, glass, and metals, can be separated from wastes and recycled, a lot of waste is still disposed of in landfill sites. Waste from nuclear power stations is reprocessed and stored in sealed containers.

◄ One of the major sources of water pollution is chemical waste from factories being discharged into rivers or lakes.

▼ Sewage, animal waste, and fertilizers can eventually kill off life in a river. Bacteria in the water use oxygen to break-down this organic waste into nutrients. The nutrients encourage the rapid growth of algae. As these die, they add to the organic waste present in the river. The bacteria use so much oxygen to break down all the organic waste that fish cannot breathe and they die.

waste is put into the water than can decay naturally, the water can become polluted with disease-carrying sewage or with products which may be poisonous to the animals and plants living in it.

Sometimes, water can be polluted by becoming too rich in nourishment, possibly from FERTILIZERS draining from agricultural land. If this happens, certain plants grow rapidly and use up all the oxygen in the water.

In many countries, waste products must be treated before they are released into seas and rivers.

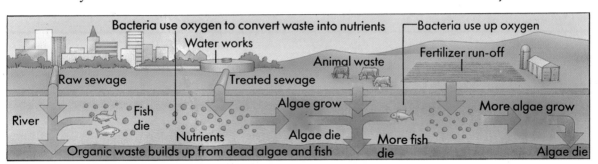

WATER

Chemically, water is a molecule consisting of two atoms of the gas hydrogen linked by chemical bonds to one atom of the gas oxygen. Pure water, at normal temperatures and pressures, is a tasteless and colorless liquid which lacks any kind of smell. The water we drink, which comes from the water supply, does have a taste because it contains minerals which have dissolved in it when it passed through rocks as groundwater. Water is a very good solvent and is able to dissolve more solids than many other liquids. Water is also good for cleaning because it dissolves dirt. Heating it and adding soap or detergent increases its efficiency. Water is the main component of blood and many substances are carried around the body in this watery liquid. Water also helps to remove some body wastes in the form of another liquid, urine. Water helps animals to keep cool because when animals sweat or pant, water evaporates, and removes some of their body heat.

Temperature changes the state of water. At temperatures above 212°F (100°C) it becomes water vapor or the gas, steam. At 32°F (0°C) water freezes to form solid ice. Most solids become denser than their liquid form when they freeze but water is at its most dense at 39°F (4°C).

Flowing water can be used to turn water wheels to provide power and in hydroelectric schemes is used to provide electricity. It circulates between the atmosphere and the Earth in a process known as the water, or hydrological, cycle.

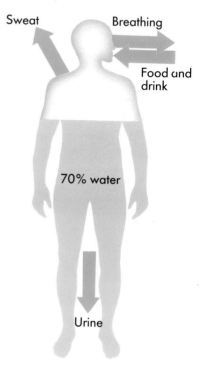

▲ Water probably has the best known chemical formula: H_2O, that is one oxygen atom and two of hydrogen. It is a remarkable substance, needed for all forms of life.

▲ A person can go without food for several weeks if necessary, but without water life cannot last more than a few days. The human body is 70 percent water. We take it in with food and drink, and lose it in urine, in sweat, and in our breath (as water vapor).

▲ Deserts have no free water in streams or lakes, and rain is very rare. There are occasional wells and wet places even in deserts and these are called oases. An oasis is therefore a welcome source of life-giving water to people and animals in these dry environments. Depending on the amount of water, an oasis may support a few families and their animals or it may support a big city.

◀ Over thousands of years, flowing water can find its way through even the hardest rocks, carving out deep canyons and gorges with its constant pressure. Here the Yellowstone River flows out of the lower (downstream) end of the Grand Canyon.

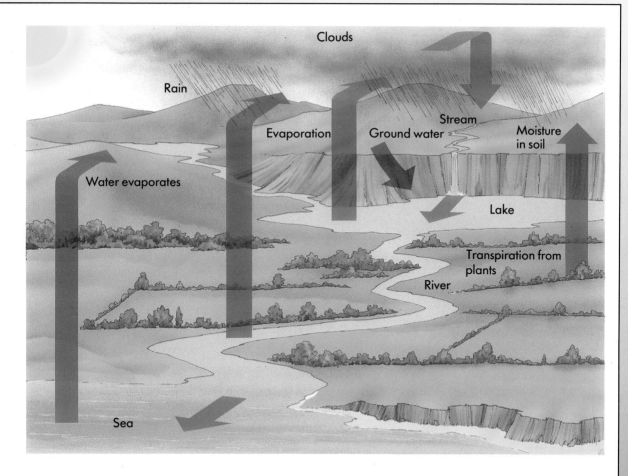

Clouds

Rain

Evaporation

Stream

Ground water

Moisture
in soil

Water evaporates

Lake

Transpiration from
plants

River

Sea

▲ All the water in the world goes around and around in a great cycle. Water that falls as rain soaks into the ground and is taken up by plants or runs off and forms rivers, which flow to the sea. Plants give off water vapor from their leaves, and water in rivers and the sea also evaporates as vapor. The vapor condenses in the atmosphere to form clouds, which produce rain to keep the cycle going.

Water is unusual in that most liquids contract as they cool and freeze, but water contracts to 39°F (4°C) and then expands as it freezes. This is important for animals because if a pond or river freezes over, the less dense ice floats, leaving liquid water beneath in which fish and other animals can survive.

SEE FOR YOURSELF

Water pressure depends on the "head" of water — the height of the top of the water supply above the level at which it is used. This is because of the pressure exerted by the volume of water above the outlet. You can show this by making a series of holes down the side of a plastic bottle. Cover the holes with tape and fill the bottle with water. Remember to place a bowl on the floor to catch the water before quickly removing the bits of tape. The jet of water where the pressure is greatest (at the bottom of the bottle) squirts out farther than water from near the top.

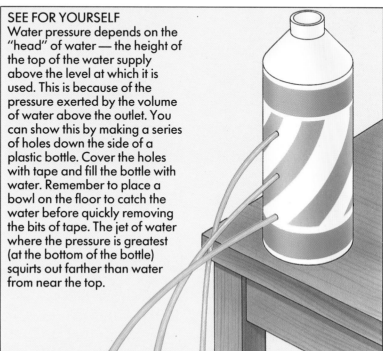

See also CLOUD; EVAPORATION; GROUNDWATER; HEAVY WATER; HYDRO-ELECTRICITY; HYDROGEN BONDS; ICE; PRECIPITATION; STEAM.

▲ In times of drought or in parts of the world where water is in short supply, it may not be possible to pipe water to people's homes. These people have to carry all the water they use from a communal pipe.

Water supply

A supply of unpolluted fresh WATER is vital for humans. Various methods are used to supply and purify water. Water may be piped from rivers which are reasonably free of POLLUTION. Such water must be filtered and treated to ensure that it is clean. For small-scale supplies, water may be obtained by drilling a well in the ground to below the level of the WATER TABLE. Sometimes GROUNDWATER may be under pressure because of the rock structure. If a well is dug into the water-bearing rocks, the water is forced to the surface under its own pressure as an ARTESIAN WELL. In areas where the population is large, hollows or river valleys may be dammed and flooded to provide reservoirs. In dry parts of the world, water may be piped, or carried in channels, over long distances to irrigate growing crops.

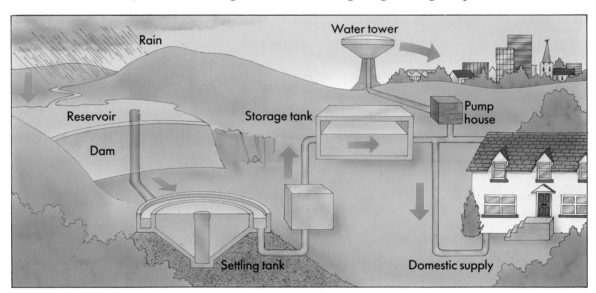

▲ Water for use in homes and factories is stored in a reservoir, often behind a dam, before being piped to a water works. At the water works, any particles in the water are allowed to settle out in settling tanks and then the water is filtered and treated with chlorine to kill any germs. In some places the purified water is supplied from tall water towers. When water needs to be moved uphill it has to be pumped to overcome gravity.

Water table

The water table is the top surface of those porous ROCKS which are saturated with GROUNDWATER. In general, the line of the water table follows that of the land surface but it rises and falls depending on the amount of PRECIPITATION that filters into the rocks and on how much WATER is drawn from them. Rock which is saturated with water is referred to as an *aquifer*. The aquifer is not a kind of underground pool. The water is held in the pores and cracks in the rocks.

The SOIL and rocks can be divided into three zones:

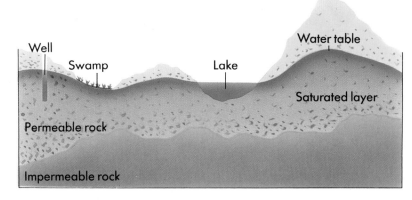

Well

Swamp

Lake

Water table

Saturated layer

Permeable rock

Impermeable rock

◄ *Water soaks into the ground until it reaches rock that is impermeable to water. The permeable rock above this becomes "filled" with water up to the level known as the water table. If this level is at the surface, the ground will be wet or swampy. A lake will tend to soak the ground beneath it and raise the water table. A well must be dug deep below the water table to stop it from drying out in a drought.*

the zone from the surface down through which water passes to reach the aquifer; the zone which is sometimes saturated; the zone which is permanently saturated, and may be 3,000 feet (1,000 m) deep. A well that will not run dry in a drought must be drilled into this last zone.

Watson, James *See* DNA

Watt

The watt (W) is the SI UNIT of POWER. One watt corresponds to the conversion of one JOULE of ENERGY from one form into another every second. For example, a light bulb uses about 100 watts of power, so it turns 100 joules of electrical energy into heat and light every second, while an electric toaster may have a power of about 1,000 watts or 1 kilowatt (kW), so it converts 1,000 joules of electrical energy into heat every second. The ENGINE of a medium-sized car produces about 50,000 watts (50 kW), while a large electrical power station produces several hundred million watts.
See also KILOWATT-HOUR.

Watt, James *See* Power

Wave

A wave is a disturbance or displacement that repeats itself. Both ELECTROMAGNETIC RADIATION, which includes LIGHT and RADIO waves, and SOUND travel as waves. The simplest kind of wave is called a sine wave. A sine wave is described by its amplitude (the height of the wave) and its WAVELENGTH. In many WAVE MOTIONS, a sine wave travels along without changing its shape at a particular VELOCITY. The number of peaks or troughs of the wave

Powerful Electricity
An electric heater converts electrical energy into heat energy. The rate at which it does this is its power. For example, if it converts 1,000 joules of electricity into heat in 1 second, its power is 1,000 joules per second or 1,000 watts (equal to 1 kilowatt).

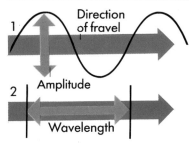

Direction of travel

1

2

Amplitude

Wavelength

▲ *The two main properties of a wave are its amplitude and wavelength. The amplitude is the maximum displacement — the height from the crest of a wave to a trough. The wavelength is the distance between two consecutive waves. The number of waves that pass a particular point in a given time gives the frequency of the waves.*

▶ *Refraction, reflection, and diffraction are all important properties of waves. Waves are refracted, or bent, when they pass from one substance into another of different density. For example, when sound waves travel from air into a brick wall, they are refracted. They are refracted back to the same original direction when they pass out of the brick and into the air again. Reflection and diffraction are other ways in which waves can be bent (see diagram). In reflection, the waves bounce off a barrier, just as a light beam bounces off a mirror. Sound echoes are produced when sound waves bounce back off a wall or cliff. In diffraction, the waves spread out after they have passed through a narrow gap in a barrier.*

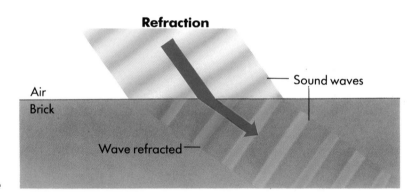

Refraction

Air
Brick

Sound waves

Wave refracted

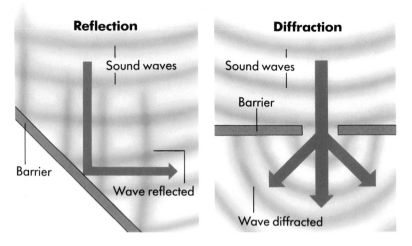

Reflection

Sound waves

Barrier

Wave reflected

Diffraction

Sound waves

Barrier

Wave diffracted

SEE FOR YOURSELF
If you take hold of the end of a length of rope and give it a quick up-and-down flick, a transverse wave will run along the rope. You can keep the waves going by keeping the end moving. You can also make waves by dropping a light ball into a bowl of water. The ripples that spread out are longitudinal waves.

Standing wave

Transverse wave

passing a point each second is the FREQUENCY of the wave.

One important property of waves is that they can "interfere;" if two waves are present in the same place at the same time, their effects add up. If the peaks of one wave arrive at a point at the same time as the peaks of the other, then they combine to give a peak twice as high. However, if the peaks of one wave arrive at an observer at the same time as the troughs of the other, they cancel each other out. Interference is important in DIFFRACTION, the way waves spread out as they pass through a narrow opening or around an obstacle.
See also REFLECTION; REFRACTION.

Wave motion

A wave motion is a pattern of disturbance that changes regularly as time passes and the wave moves from one place to another. The disturbance might be in the position of the surface of a liquid, as in waves on the sea, or in the PRESSURE of a gas, as in a SOUND wave in air, or in the electrical and magnetic fields, as in a LIGHT wave. Waves can be divided into traveling waves which move

◄ *A water droplet hitting the surface of water causes longitudinal waves that travel out in widening circles from where the drop landed. Two drops of water will each produce waves or ripples which will interfere with each other when they meet.*

Waves can also travel through solid material. If something is hit or twisted, it vibrates. The vibrations are waves that travel through the material. Earthquakes are waves traveling through solid rocks of the Earth. The denser the rocks, the faster the waves travel. Such waves can travel at several miles per second.

along with time, like a sound wave in the open air, or standing waves which stay in the same place like the waves on a drumhead when it is struck. They can also be divided into longitudinal waves, such as sound in a FLUID, where the wave disturbance flows in the same direction as the wave, and transverse waves such as light where the disturbance flows at right angles to the direction of travel.

See also FREQUENCY; WAVE; WAVELENGTH.

Wave power

Where the vibration is at right angles to the direction the wave is moving, the wave is a **transverse wave**. When the vibration is in the same direction as the direction of the wave, the wave is a **longitudinal wave**.

Wave power describes the production of ELECTRICITY from the motion of waves at sea. As waves travel along the sea's surface, the water at any point on the surface does not travel with the wave. It moves up and down. This motion can be used to drive GENERATORS. Several types of wave-power generator have been designed and built. The best-known is the "nodding duck." A line of floats are each pivoted at one side, allowing the other side to nod up and down with the waves. The hub where each float pivots contains a water pump. The pump, driven by the nodding action of

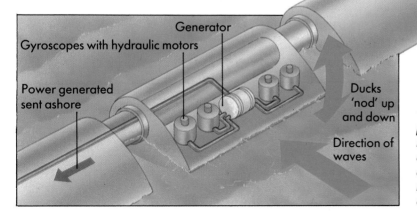

Gyroscopes with hydraulic motors

Generator

Power generated sent ashore

Ducks 'nod' up and down

Direction of waves

◄ *One method of generating power from sea waves uses rows of floats called nodding ducks. As the floats bob up and down, the energy in their movement is used to generate electricity.*

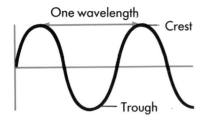

▲ *Wavelength is the distance between two waves.*

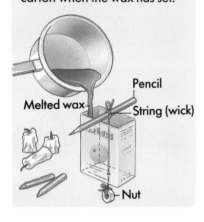

▼ *Honeybees make wax to build the comb in which they raise their grubs inside the hive.*

the float, pumps water through the float. The flow of this pumped water is used to power a TURBINE which drives a generator.
See also ENERGY; TIDAL POWER.

Wavelength

A wave is a disturbance that repeats itself in space; the wavelength is the distance between two similar places on the wave at one TIME; for example, it is the distance between one wave peak and the next. The wavelength, multiplied by the FREQUENCY of the wave, gives the wave's VELOCITY. This means that if two different sorts of ELECTROMAGNETIC RADIATION travel at the same velocity, the waves with higher frequency have shorter wavelengths and the waves with lower frequency have longer wavelengths. For example, a RADIO wave might have a frequency of 200 kHz (a kHz is one thousand cycles per second) and a wavelength of 1,500 m, while a light wave might have a frequency of 600 THz (600 million million hertz) and a wavelength of 500 nm (500 millionths of a millimeter). Both have the same wave velocity.

Wax

A wax is a solid or semisolid substance obtained from living things or from MINERAL sources. Examples include beeswax from the honeycomb of a beehive; tallow made from suet, which is the FAT inside animals such as cattle and sheep; and paraffin wax made from crude oil. Waxes are characterized by being insoluble in water, and by softening or melting when heated. Today, synthetic waxes are manufactured by the PLASTICS industry. Waxes repel water and have many uses. They are used to coat paper and leather to make them waterproof. They are also made into furniture polishes, candles, crayons, cosmetics, and ointments, and used in making matches and electrical INSULATORS.

Weather

Weather is the name given to the combination of the changing conditions of the ATMOSPHERE, including temperature, PRECIPITATION, atmospheric pressure, HUMIDITY, hours of sunshine, the amount and type of CLOUDS, and the speed and direction of the WIND. In some parts of

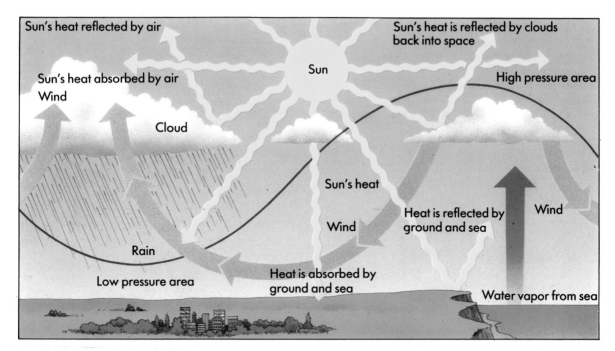

Labels within diagram:

Sun's heat reflected by air

Sun's heat is reflected by clouds back into space

Sun

Sun's heat absorbed by air

Wind

High pressure area

Cloud

Sun's heat

Wind

Heat is reflected by ground and sea

Wind

Rain

Low pressure area

Heat is absorbed by ground and sea

Water vapor from sea

the world, such as western Australia, the weather may be the same week after week and month after month. Elsewhere, the weather is very unstable, and may change from hour to hour.

Weather is not the same as CLIMATE. Climate is the average weather of an area over a long period of time. The weather may change from day to day and is a mixture of many things. Some of these scientists understand, others are still a mystery. Nearly all weather occurs in the lowest layer of the atmosphere — the troposphere — and depends on four elements — temperature, wind, air pressure, and moisture. The boundary between two different air masses is called a FRONT and it is these fronts, moving across a region, which give rise to the type of weather.

Weather forecasting *See* Meteorology

Weathering *See* Erosion and Weathering

Weight

Weight is the downward FORCE which acts on all objects because they are attracted by GRAVITY toward the center of the EARTH. The weight of an object depends on its MASS; an object with twice the mass has twice the weight, so an object's weight can be used to measure its

▲ *Weather is produced by the heat of the Sun and the effects it has on the atmosphere. The Sun's heat causes water to evaporate. The water vapor forms clouds in the atmosphere, which give rain or snow. Heat from the Sun warms the air, which rises, creating areas of low pressure. Wind is air moving from high-pressure areas to low-pressure areas.*

Weather Facts
The heaviest **rainstorm** occurred on the island of Réunion which in 1952 had 74 inches (1,870 mm) of rain in 24 hours. The driest place on Earth is Arica in Chile which averages only three-hundredth inch (0.76 mm) of rain per year. The highest **temperature** recorded was 136°F (58°C) in the shade in Libya in 1922. The lowest temperature was −129°F (−89.2°C) at Vostok in Antarctica in 1983. The strongest wind was 231 mph at Mt. Washington in 1934.

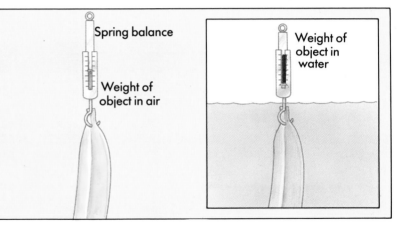

Spring balance

Weight of object in air

Weight of object in water

▶ *The mass of an object is constant but its weight depends on the force of gravity. 1 A person who weighs 150 pounds (68 kg) on Earth weighs only 24 pounds (11 kg) on the Moon 2, because the Moon's gravity is one-sixth of Earth's. The same person in a spaceship accelerating through space would feel weightless 3.*

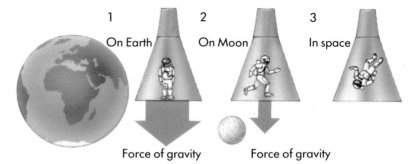

| 1 | 2 | 3 |
| On Earth | On Moon | In space |

Force of gravity   Force of gravity

mass. However, the mass and the weight are not the same; the mass depends only on the amount of material in the object and would be the same no matter where the object was taken in the universe. The weight, however, depends on which other masses are nearby. For example, at the surface of the Moon the weight of an object is about one-sixth of its weight on the Earth because the force of gravity on the MOON is much less than that on Earth. Astronauts in a spacecraft orbiting the Earth feel no weight. They are free of the effects of the pull of the Earth's gravity. There is no up or down. This is just like the sudden lessening in your weight that you feel when you stand in an elevator which starts to move downward. But your mass remains constant.

Weights and Measures

Many things in life depend on our ability to measure things accurately and meaningfully. Think of all the different things that you do that require some form of MEASUREMENT. Going on a trip requires a knowledge of distance and time, buying a rug requires a knowledge of area, drawing a triangle requires a knowledge of angles, etc. But it is not just the measuring that is

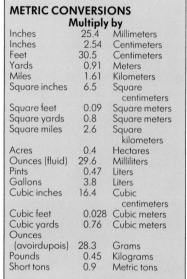

◄ *The best way of selling similar things of different sizes is by weight. Simple balances like this one have been used for thousands of years to weigh objects for sale.*

METRIC CONVERSIONS		
Multiply by		
Inches	25.4	Millimeters
Inches	2.54	Centimeters
Feet	30.5	Centimeters
Yards	0.91	Meters
Miles	1.61	Kilometers
Square inches	6.5	Square centimeters
Square feet	0.09	Square meters
Square yards	0.8	Square meters
Square miles	2.6	Square kilometers
Acres	0.4	Hectares
Ounces (fluid)	29.6	Milliliters
Pints	0.47	Liters
Gallons	3.8	Liters
Cubic inches	16.4	Cubic centimeters
Cubic feet	0.028	Cubic meters
Cubic yards	0.76	Cubic meters
Ounces (avoirdupois)	28.3	Grams
Pounds	0.45	Kilograms
Short tons	0.9	Metric tons

important, it is the use of the most sensible units that matters. You would not measure the distance between two towns using a 12 in ruler, but you might if the two towns were on a MAP.

Scientists throughout the world use the same units of length, time, mass, and so on. These are called SI UNITS after the French for International System of Units. Using this system, a measurement made in any country uses the same units as those used in any other country.

Today, nearly the whole world uses the metric system. In 1901 the U.S. National Bureau of Standards was established to regulate standard measure. But it was only in the 1970s that the United States and Canada began introducing the metric system.

Weismann, A. *See* Chromosomes and Genes

Welding

Welding is used to join METAL objects by melting their edges so that they fuse together. There are several welding methods: forge welding, OXYACETYLENE WELDING, ELECTRIC ARC welding, seam welding, and spot welding. In forge welding, the parts are heated and then hammered together. Oxyacetylene welding uses a gas flame to heat the parts. In electric arc welding, the metal forms one electrode of an electric CIRCUIT and a metal rod called a filler rod forms the second electrode. When the two electrodes are held close together a spark jumps

▲ *Construction workers use oxyacetylene torches to cut and weld steel girders. Joints in sheet metal, such as for car body repairs, are usually made by electric arc welding.*

753

▲ *George Westinghouse is best known for his invention of the air brake used in railroad locomotives and vehicles.*

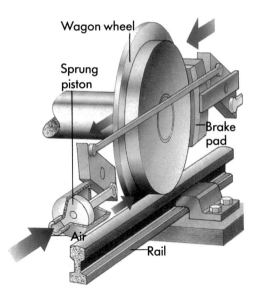

Wagon wheel

Sprung piston

Brake pad

Air

Rail

▲ *The Westinghouse brake uses air pressure to move a piston against the pressure of a spring. Movement of the piston works a lever that forces the brake pad against the edge of the wheel.*

▶ *A white dwarf is a star in the final stage of its life. A medium-sized star, like our Sun, gradually swells as it ages to become a red giant. The giant's outer material escapes into space, and its core shrinks to form a white dwarf.*

from one to the other, melting both the metal parts and the filler rod. Spot and seam welding are both electrical methods. The joint is clamped between two electrodes and a current is passed through it. The electrical RESISTANCE of the metal causes it to heat up until it melts.

Westinghouse, George

George Westinghouse (1846–1914) was the U.S. inventor and industrialist responsible for the use of alternating current (AC) for electrical supply in the United States. Westinghouse imported an AC system from Britain and developed it further. He employed the engineer Nikola Tesla to perfect it. After a struggle between AC and DC supporters, AC was eventually adopted.

In the 1860s Westinghouse produced a series of INVENTIONS ranging from a rotary STEAM ENGINE to his first major invention in 1869, the air brake. The Westinghouse air brake was widely used by railroads in the United States. He went on to improve the design so that it worked automatically. He later developed a new railroad signaling system and then patented several dozen original ideas for piping NATURAL GAS.

White dwarf

A white dwarf is the final stage of a normal STAR like our SUN, before it fades into blackness. It is the remains of the star's core, where the NUCLEAR ENERGY that made the star shine was generated. A white dwarf is made when a RED GIANT collapses at its center. Although made of hydrogen and helium, which we know as gases, the atoms in a white dwarf are compressed so tightly that they are hundreds of times denser than lead. The surface is about 14,000°F (8,000°C), but white dwarfs are so small they send out little light, and are hard to detect.

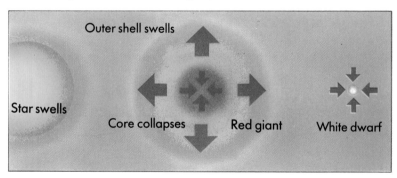

Outer shell swells

Star swells

Core collapses

Red giant

White dwarf

Whittle, Frank *See* Jet propulsion

Wind

Wind is the movement of AIR which depends upon variations in atmospheric PRESSURE. Air normally flows from areas of high atmospheric pressure to areas of low atmospheric pressure. In other words, if the EARTH did not spin on its axis, wind would normally blow from high to low pressure areas. But because the planet spins from west to east the winds are deflected to the right in the Northern HEMISPHERE and to the left in the Southern Hemisphere. This is the Coriolis effect and, in the north, it means that the airflow is clockwise around an area of high pressure and counterclockwise around an area of low pressure and in the South, the other way around.

The speed of the wind depends on the differences in the air pressures. If you look at a weather map, the winds

▲ Trees that grow in places where there is a strong wind that usually comes from one direction grow crookedly, leaning away from the wind. The wind on the seashore usually comes from the sea.

Beaufort Wind Scale
The force of the wind can be expressed on the Beaufort wind scale, which defines wind strength in terms of the wind's effects on objects in its path. The scale was devised by the British admiral Sir Francis Beaufort in 1805. The Beaufort scale is a series of numbers from 0 (no wind) to 12 (a violent hurricane). The steps on the scale are:
0 Calm (less than 1 mph). Smoke rises straight up.
1–3 Light wind (up to 12 mph). Leaves and twigs move, flags blow out.
4–5 Moderate wind (up to 24 mph). Small trees sway, waves on lakes.
6–7 Strong wind (up to 38 mph). Large trees sway, and walking is hard.
8–9 Gale (up to 54 mph). Shingles fall off roofs.
10–11 Storm (up to 73 mph). Widespread damage is caused to buildings and property.
12 Hurricane (over 73 mph). Devastation.

Force 0
Force 1–3
Force 4–5
Force 6–7
Force 8–9
Force 10–11
Force 12

▼ The general directions of winds around the world follow a simple pattern. The directions of these winds is affected by the motion of the Earth spinning on its axis. They tend to blow in a southwesterly direction in the Northern Hemisphere and northwesterly in the Southern Hemisphere. There is little wind in the doldrums on either side of the equator.

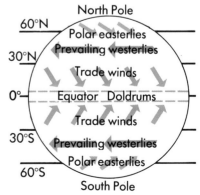

North Pole
60°N Polar easterlies
Prevailing westerlies
30°N
Trade winds
0° Equator Doldrums
Trade winds
30°S Prevailing westerlies
Polar easterlies
60°S
South Pole

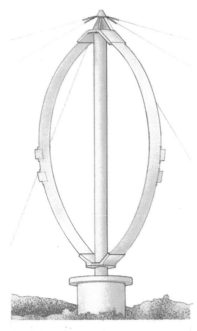

will be strongest where the ISOBARS (lines of equal pressure) are closer together. Wind speed is measured using an ANEMOMETER. The speed or force of the wind may be measured by a scale of numbers from 1 to 12. This is referred to as the Beaufort scale.

Wind power

Wind power describes the ways in which the ENERGY of the WIND can be harnessed, usually to generate ELECTRICITY. It is one of the various kinds of alternative energy sources. One of the benefits of wind power is that it generates energy without any POLLUTION.

In flat countries such as the Netherlands, where the wind can blow without interruption, people have used windmills to grind their corn or to pump water from the ground for many years. Some countries build very large wind generators called wind turbines, where one GENER-

▲ *One design for a modern windmill has two curved blades that spin on a vertical axis. Strong cables act as guy ropes to anchor the mill and keep it upright.*

▶ *Windmills called bonnet mills, which have a "cap" that moves around so that the sails always face the wind, were once common in the Netherlands. Most of them were used for pumping water, not for grinding corn.*

SEE FOR YOURSELF
You can make a pinwheel from thin cardboard to show how a windmill works. Cut out a four-pointed star as shown, making sure that the hole is exactly in the middle. Fold over the edges to form vanes, and use a thumbtack to fix the cardboard to a wooden handle. Either put the windmill upright in the ground or on a post, or swing it around at arm's length to create a flow of air over the vanes.

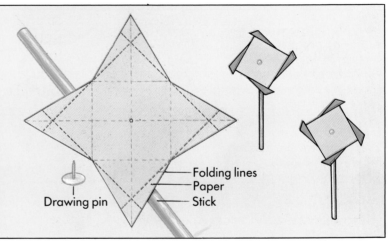

Drawing pin

Folding lines
Paper
Stick

◀ A collection of modern windmills make up a "wind farm" in California. The windmills drive generators that produce electricity.

ATOR can generate enough electricity for the local people in rural areas. In other places "wind farms" of many wind turbines are constructed in isolated open areas. These turbines have large blades set on a horizontal shaft and mounted on a tall mast.

Wind tunnel

A wind tunnel is a device used to study the way that AIR flows around objects. Powerful engines generate a constant flow of air through the tunnel and around test objects inside it. Sensors attached to the objects reveal whether the airflow is smooth or turbulent and measures forces such as lift and drag generated by the airflow.

Aircraft manufacturers test models of new aircraft in wind tunnels as do car manufacturers because streamlined vehicles use less FUEL. Architects test models of bridges and buildings to make sure that they are stable in high winds.

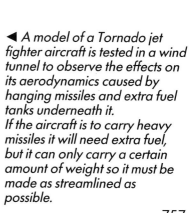

▲ The most efficient modern wind machines have two or three blades like the propeller of an aircraft. An electricity generator is located inside the "head" of the machine. The head can also rotate to keep the blades pointed into the wind.

◀ A model of a Tornado jet fighter aircraft is tested in a wind tunnel to observe the effects on its aerodynamics caused by hanging missiles and extra fuel tanks underneath it.
If the aircraft is to carry heavy missiles it will need extra fuel, but it can only carry a certain amount of weight so it must be made as streamlined as possible.

▲ A cable contains many wires, all carrying different currents. Cables such as this are commonly used for carrying communications signals, such as telephone messages. Each separate wire in the cable is surrounded by insulation material which is usually plastic. This is to stop the current from jumping from wire to wire.

The largest wind tunnel in the world is operated by the U.S. space agency, NASA, in California. Its six engines can produce air speeds of up to 345 mph (555 km/h). *See also* AERODYNAMICS; STREAMLINING.

Wire

Wire is a flexible, fine strand of metal. A cable made from a number of metal strands twisted together is also called wire. Wire for electrical purposes is made from a good CONDUCTOR of electricity such as copper.

The electrical conductor is usually covered with a coating of plastic or enamel called a sleeve to insulate it from other conductors. A cable may contain a number of individual wires, each with its own plastic sleeve. The plastic sleeves may be color-coded to identify which wire does what in a CIRCUIT. Main electrical wiring, for example, is coded so that it can be connected correctly and safely to plugs and household appliances.

Wire is made by pulling metal rods through a series of progressively smaller holes in metal blocks called dies in a process called drawing.

All wood decay is caused by bacteria and fungi. They eat into the cells and leave rotting wood behind. If they were deprived of oxygen, heat, and moisture, they could not exist and the wood would last indefinitely. Some piles that Julius Caesar used in bridges in France were found to be sound after 2,000 years.

Wood

Wood is the tough material that forms trunks and branches of trees. The same material also occurs in smaller amounts in the ROOTS and STEMS of other plants. It consists of tough-walled tubes and fibers in the plant's xylem. The tubes carry water and mineral salts up the trunk to the LEAVES, while the fibers provide the additional strength necessary to support the trunk and branches. The tubes and fibers start out as living CELLS, but a CARBOHYDRATE called lignin soon begins to build

▶ The wood in a tree trunk forms in layers which appear as rings if the trunk is cut through. Beneath the outer bark is a layer of sapwood containing rings of phloem and xylem vessels. These are made up of tiny tubes and run the length of the trunk to carry food and water to the branches and leaves. A new ring of wood is formed each year and so it is possible to tell the age of a tree by counting the rings. The hard dry center of the trunk is called heartwood.

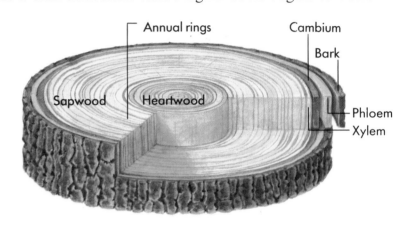

Annual rings — Cambium — Bark — Sapwood — Heartwood — Phloem — Xylem

up in their walls and make them hard. The cells then die, although they still work in the same way.

A tree trunk grows thicker by producing a new ring of wood just under the bark every year. The rings are clearly marked in trees growing in cool regions, where growth stops in the winter. They are called annual rings and are less obvious in tropical trees, which generally grow throughout the year. The oldest wood in the center of the trunk gradually gets crushed and cannot carry water. It is called heartwood and is usually harder and darker than the wood on the outside. This younger wood, which still carries water, is called sapwood.

Large areas of the world used to be covered with trees but today they are being cut down for FUEL, to make PAPER, and to clear land for farming.
See also DEFORESTATION; DENDROCHRONOLOGY.

Word processor

A word processor is a COMPUTER designed to be used for creating, editing, and storing text. At any time, the text may be retrieved from the word processor's memory and printed. A word processor consists of a keyboard similar to a typewriter keyboard, a VISUAL DISPLAY UNIT for displaying the text, a computer dedicated to processing text, a memory device such as a disk drive, and a printer. The disk drive stores the text on magnetic disks until it is needed again. A microcomputer with a word processing program can be used as a word processor.

Text is entered on the keyboard. After it has been

SEE FOR YOURSELF
You may be able to use a word processor at home or at school. Try writing a letter to a friend using a word processor. When you have written it, correct any mistakes you have made. Check that all of your spelling is correct — the word processor may be able to do this for you! Then see if you can improve the letter by making changes to it.

▼ *In many offices that deal with large amounts of text, several word processors can be linked to a central data bank as a network. In a network, several word processors can use the same printer.*

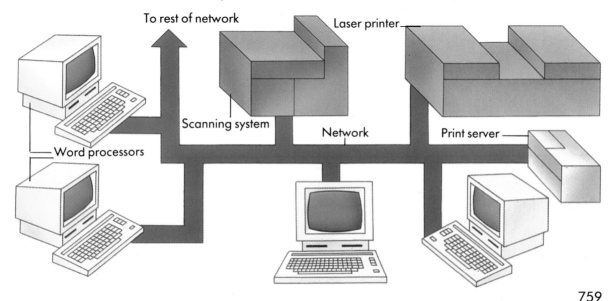

To rest of network · Laser printer · Scanning system · Network · Print server · Word processors

▲ *Work is done when a force makes something move in the direction of the force. Pushing a car along involves work, but holding a book does not because the book is not being moved.*

▼ *In a steam locomotive, work is done by steam pressure because it makes the pistons move. The heat energy of the steam is converted into the mechanical energy of the moving piston. But some energy is wasted as work that has to be done to overcome friction in the moving parts.*

entered, it can be changed, corrected, and moved on the screen before printing. Some word processors can incorporate graphics to produce illustrated documents. *See also* COMPUTER GRAPHICS; HARDWARE; SOFTWARE.

Work

In PHYSICS, work is said to be done when an object on which a FORCE is acting moves in the direction of that force. For example, if you are helping to push a car from the back and the car moves forward, you do work on the car. On the other hand, if you are standing still holding a heavy book in your hands, you do not do any work on it since the book is not moving. Similarly, if you are pushing the car from the side, even if the car moves forward (not sideways), you do not do any work because the car did not move in the same direction that you were pushing.

Work is the way in which ENERGY is changed from one form into another; having a certain amount of energy means that you are able to do a certain amount of work. Work and energy are both measured in JOULES. For example, when pushing the car, chemical energy stored in your body goes into doing work, which increases the kinetic energy of the car. Machines are designed to make the best use of the work that is done by reducing the FRICTION forces, the amount of kinetic energy lost or wasted as HEAT, and so on.

▶ *The work done in using a wrench is equal to the force applied to the handle multiplied by the distance the handle moves in the direction of the force.*

Work (effort)

Steam in   Steam out

Pistons

Work (effort)

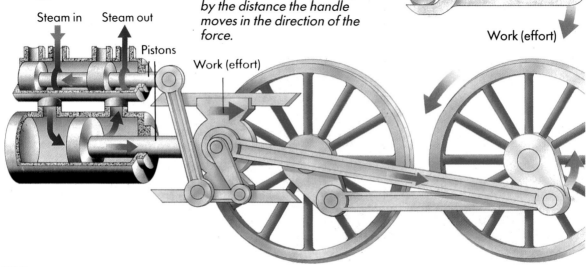

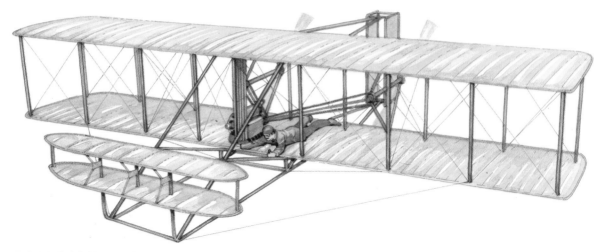

▲ *The world's first successful powered airplane, Flyer I (above) was built after experimenting with gliders (left).*

Wright, Orville and Wilbur

Wilbur Wright (1867–1912) and his brother Orville (1871–1948) made the world's first controlled flight of a powered airplane in 1903. The two brothers were interested in machines and designed and made printing presses and bicycles.

Between 1900 and 1902 they built a series of gliders to test the controls that would be used in their next venture, the powered airplane called Flyer I. Its historic flight on December 17, 1903 at Kill Devil Hills, Kitty Hawk, North Carolina lasted 12 seconds. They went on to build more airplanes, improving the design each time. They had to design and make their own propellers and ENGINES because none that was suitable existed at the time. Wilbur demonstrated their airplanes in Europe in 1908 and 1909, while Orville built the first airplane for the U.S. Army.

See also FLIGHT.

▲ *The Wright brothers, Wilbur (top) and Orville (bottom) played an important part in the development of aircraft.*

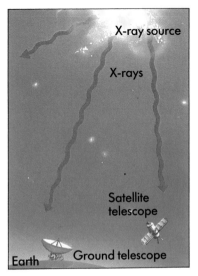

Xerography *See* Photocopier

X-ray astronomy

All STARS send out a wide range of ELECTROMAGNETIC RADIATION from their surfaces, including X-RAYS, but the strongest radiation is in the visible part of the SPECTRUM. The hottest stars, however, send out large amounts of X-rays, which cannot be seen and cannot penetrate the ATMOSPHERE. X-ray astronomy is carried out by SATELLITES, such as ROSAT, launched in 1990.

To produce X-rays in a star, temperatures of at least a million degrees are needed. The Sun's core (about 27 million°F) produces them, and they would gradually destroy our CELLS if the atmosphere did not protect us.

There are many very bright X-ray objects in the sky: SUPERNOVAE, WHITE DWARFS, QUASARS, and NEUTRON STARS all send out X-rays. Some PULSARS also emit them, as do BLACK HOLES such as Cygnus X-1.

▲ *X-rays from sources in space cannot be detected by telescopes on Earth. The first satellite to carry X-ray detectors was launched by the Soviet Union in 1958.*

X-ray diffraction

X-ray diffraction is used to discover how the ATOMS of a CRYSTAL are arranged. The atoms of a crystal lie in orderly rows. The spaces between the rows bend, or diffract, beams of X-rays. In 1912 the German physicist Max von Laue used a crystal to diffract X-rays, for which he received the NOBEL Prize in Physics in 1914. The pattern of intense spots made on photographic film by diffracted X-rays gives information about the crystal's structure. The relationship between the spots and the

Sir William Henry Bragg (1862–1942) and Sir William Lawrence Bragg (1890–1971)
The Braggs, father (left) and son, were British physicists who developed the technique of X-ray diffraction to investigate crystals. When they aimed a beam of X-rays at a crystal, the regular arrangement of atoms in the crystal scattered the X-rays to produce a characteristic pattern on a photographic plate. They shared the 1915 Nobel Prize in Physics.

spacing of atoms in the crystal was discovered by the two physicists, William and Lawrence Bragg. X-ray diffraction was used by Crick, Watson, and Wilkins to find the structure of the genetic material, DNA.

X-rays

X-rays are one kind of ELECTROMAGNETIC RADIATION. They have a very high FREQUENCY of about a million million million hertz (cycles per second), and so a very short WAVELENGTH. They were discovered in 1895 by Wilhelm Roentgen; he gave them their name because the letter X is often used to stand for something unknown. Materials which contain only light atoms do not absorb many X-rays. For example, they pass easily through most living tissue, but not through BONES which contain heavier atoms. This means that X-rays can be used to find what is wrong with bones and teeth inside the body without surgery. Because X-rays are a form of ionizing RADIATION, which can damage cells, the amount that a person receives has to be carefully controlled. X-rays are used to study the structure of SOLIDS in X-RAY DIFFRACTION, and in X-RAY ASTRONOMY.

X-rays can be produced by bombarding atoms with fast particles and knocking ELECTRONS out from the "shells" near the middle of the atom. Other electrons move in from the outer shells to take the place of the missing electrons, giving out ENERGY as X-rays.

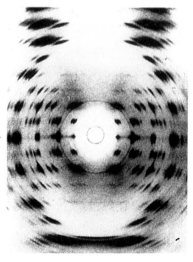

▲ X-ray diffraction is used to discover the structure of complicated molecules. This pattern is produced by DNA, which makes up genes and chromosomes in the cell nucleus.

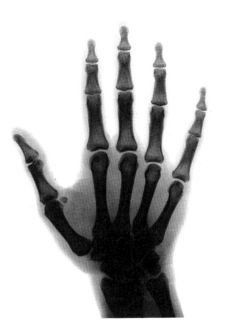

◀ Modern medical X-ray photographs, using carefully controlled doses of X-rays, can reveal the structure of soft tissues as well as hard tissues such as bone.

▼ X-rays form the part of the electromagnetic spectrum beyond ultraviolet rays. At very short wavelengths, they become gamma rays.

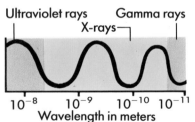

Ultraviolet rays   Gamma rays
X-rays

10^{-8} 10^{-9} 10^{-10} 10^{-11}
Wavelength in meters

Wilhelm Conrad Roentgen (1845–1923)
Roentgen was a German physicist. In 1895 he noticed that rays from a covered cathode-ray tube (which would emit no cathode rays) caused a phosphorescent screen to fluoresce. He deduced that this was caused by a new type of radiation, which he called X-rays. For this work, he received the first Nobel Prize for Physics in 1901.

Yeast

Yeasts are tiny single-celled MICROORGANISMS that are part of the group called fungi. They reproduce asexually, by budding off tiny CELLS which grow and eventually reproduce themselves. Some yeasts live naturally on the body, and they may cause DISEASE, such as thrush also known as candida, which can affect the mouth and sex organs. Yeasts also grow naturally on the surface of FRUIT, feeding on the SUGARS the fruit contains.

Some yeasts are essential in the process of FERMENTATION. When these yeasts grow in the presence of sugar, they break the sugar down to produce ethanol, a simple ALCOHOL, and release carbon dioxide. We make use of this property when making alcoholic drinks like wine and beer; the yeast ferments fruit sugars to make wine, or malt sugars, present in grain, to make beer. Yeast is also useful in baking, where the carbon dioxide gas it produces causes bread to rise. Yeast is a valuable source of PROTEIN and some VITAMINS of the B group. There are more than 600 species of yeasts.

See also BIOTECHNOLOGY; GENETIC ENGINEERING.

Dough fermented with yeast is called *leaven*. The name comes from the Latin word meaning "to raise," because fermented dough rises. Bread made of fermented dough is called leavened bread. The old English word for leaven is *yeast*.

SEE FOR YOURSELF
To watch yeast ferment, add a spoonful of sugar to a measuring cup of warm milk. Stir in some baker's yeast (or dried yeast), put the measuring cup in a warm place. A few hours later the milk will froth over as the yeast breaks down the sugar to release carbon dioxide gas.

Live yeast

Warm milk

► *Seen using an electron microscope, baker's yeast is revealed as a single-celled fungus. It is used in making bread, where the carbon dioxide produced by fermentation makes the bread rise. Yeast is also used in the production of beer and wine, where it converts the sugar from the fruit, hops, or barley into carbon dioxide and alcohol.*

Zinc

Zinc is a bluish gray ELEMENT. It is a METAL, and has been known and used for hundreds of years. Its main use today is in GALVANIZING steel. The steel is covered with zinc either by being dipped or by ELECTROLYSIS to form a protective coating that prevents the steel from rusting. Galvanized steel is used in roofing and to make water tanks. Zinc is also used to make BATTERIES.

Zinc is a part of various ALLOYS, such as brass (zinc

◄ Zinc is a metal with many uses, chief of which is in galvanizing steel. It is also made into the outer cases of dry batteries. The chief zinc alloy is brass, although other alloys are used in machines and to make coins.

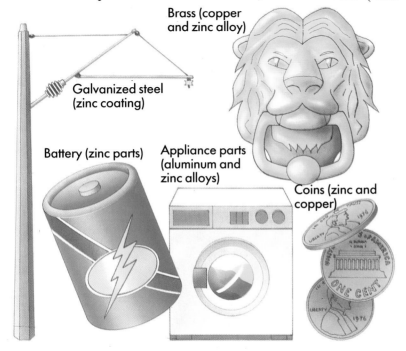

Brass (copper and zinc alloy)

Galvanized steel (zinc coating)

Battery (zinc parts)

Appliance parts (aluminum and zinc alloys)

Coins (zinc and copper)

▲ Zinc is a metal element. Like most metals it is shiny in its pure form but is only found in nature as zinc compounds.

and copper) and the zinc-based alloy (with aluminum and copper) used for casting objects such as pots and door handles. Zinc oxide is the PIGMENT known as Chinese white and is used in antiseptic ointments. Zinc sulfide glows when hit by ULTRAVIOLET light or X-RAYS and is used to coat the inside of TELEVISION screens and in luminous dials on clocks.

See also CORROSION; IRON AND STEEL; LUMINESCENCE.

Zoology

Zoology is the study of animals, from amoeba and other single-celled protozoans to humans and the huge whales. It covers the structure of the animals and their internal workings as well as the way in which they behave and how they live. *See* pages 766 and 767.

> Zinc was used by the Romans more than 2,000 years ago, but because it is always found in combination with other elements, it was not identified as a separate metal until the 1500s by the Swiss doctor Paracelsus.

ZOOLOGY

Zoology is a very large subject because there are over a million known animal species living everywhere on the Earth. Most zoologists specialize in one particular topic, such as physiology, which is the study of the processes of the animals' lives including their respiration, how they get rid of waste, how they reproduce, and so on. Others may study a particular group of animals. Entomologists, for example, study insects and ornithologists study birds. Many entomologists are involved with the control of insect pests, such as mosquitoes and locusts. Many other zoologists work in agriculture and in veterinary medicine, breeding animals for our farms and learning how to prevent and cure their various illnesses.

Ecology deals with the ways in which animals fit into their environments. It is very important for us to find out exactly what conditions the animals need if we are to conserve them in the wild. Sometimes animal species are threatened in their natural habitat and so a small population of them is preserved in a zoo or wildlife park. Some countries have game reserves or large national parks set aside for animals to live in without the interference of humans.

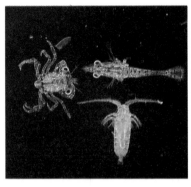

▲ Some of the smallest of the world's animals make up the plankton that lives on and near the surface of the seas. This sample includes minute copepods and the larvae of crustaceans such as crabs and shrimps. Marine plankton are the starting point for a huge number of food chains. Many fish and birds eat plankton. Even some whales exist by sieving huge quantities of minute plankton from the Antarctic waters.

▼ There are more than 80,000 species of birds in the world, from flightless penguins to high-flying vultures, and aquatic ducks and geese.

▼ Frogs are amphibians. Like toads, newts, and salamanders, they lay their eggs in water but their tadpolelike larvae change into land animals.

▼ The blue whale is a mammal that lives in the sea and is the world's largest animal. It may grow to more than 100 feet in length and weigh over 100 tons.

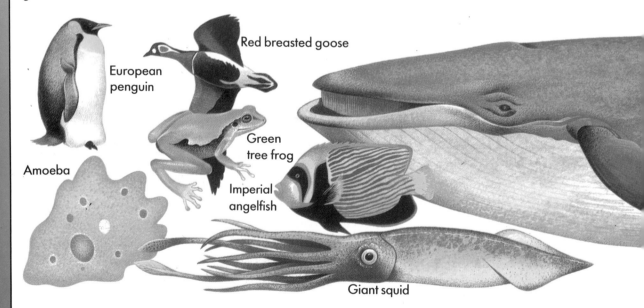

Red breasted goose

European penguin

Green tree frog

Amoeba

Imperial angelfish

Giant squid

▲ An amoeba is a microscopic single-celled animal whose jellylike body engulfs its food and pulls it inside to digest it. There are many other microscopic animals

▲ Fishes are the largest group of backboned animals (vertebrates), with about 20,000 different species varying in size from a tenth of an inch to 40 feet.

▲ The giant squid is the largest of the animals without backbones (invertebrates). It is a cephalopod which grows up to 50 feet long (including its tentacles).

► *Zoologists study the territories of birds, their population changes, and how they migrate by banding them. Here a sedge warbler is having a band put on its leg. Each band carries the address of the national organization that coordinates the information about birds that are found. A record card is filled in for each bird banded, with its weight, wing length, and species and the card is sent to the national organization and kept in case the bird is caught or found again.*

Zoologists are always making fascinating discoveries. Until recently it was thought that insects blundered into spiders' webs by accident. But it was recently discovered that some spider webs reflect ultraviolet light which attracts insects to them.

SEE FOR YOURSELF
How many worms are there in a square yard of lawn? More than you think! To find out, use string to peg out a measured square yard and, toward sunset, water the grass with dilute dishwashing liquid. This will bring the worms to the surface. When it is dark, go out with a flashlight and collect the worms in a bowl. Release them after you have counted them.

▼ *The goliath beetle is the size of a man's fist and is one of the heaviest insects in the world (some moths are larger). Insects are part of a larger group, the Arthropods.*

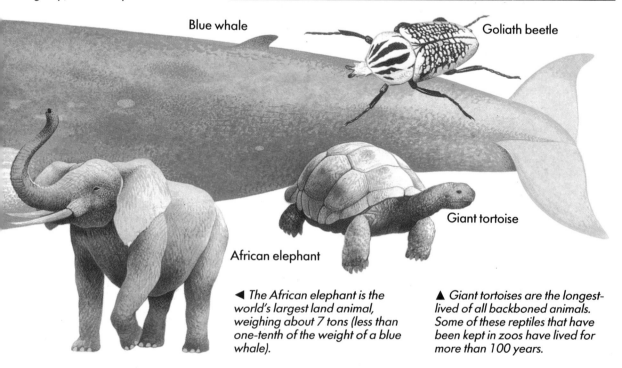

Blue whale

Goliath beetle

Giant tortoise

African elephant

◄ *The African elephant is the world's largest land animal, weighing about 7 tons (less than one-tenth of the weight of a blue whale).*

▲ *Giant tortoises are the longest-lived of all backboned animals. Some of these reptiles that have been kept in zoos have lived for more than 100 years.*

See also AGRICULTURE; BIOLOGY; BOTANY; BREEDING; CLASSIFICATION; CONSERVATION, ENVIRONMENTAL; ECOLOGY; ORGANISM; SPECIES.

Zygote

When an ovum or EGG cell is fertilized by a sperm, it produces a zygote. This single CELL holds genes from both parents, and contains all of the instructions needed to make a complete organism, with all its organs and structure preplanned. The human zygote, for example, holds genes such as those which determine if the child will have blue or brown eyes, or dark or fair hair.

The zygote stays as one cell for only a very short time, because it begins to divide and this quickly leads to the next stage in development, called a blastula.

It is a zygote which is produced by test-tube FERTILIZATION when helping couples who have been unsuccessful in having children. The sperm fertilizes an ovum which has been removed from a woman's ovary. The blastula, consisting of several cells, is implanted back into the woman to continue its development normally.

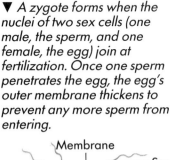

▼ A zygote forms when the nuclei of two sex cells (one male, the sperm, and one female, the egg) join at fertilization. Once one sperm penetrates the egg, the egg's outer membrane thickens to prevent any more sperm from entering.

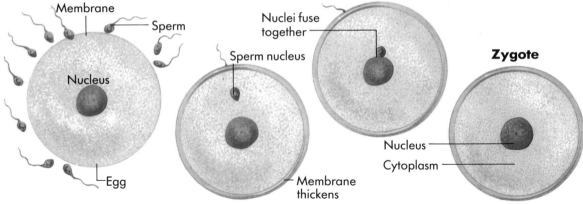

▶ A crowd of human sperm, (colored blue), try to penetrate the outer membrane of an egg, (colored yellow). The sperm look roughly spherical because their long tails do not show up on this electron microscope photograph. If a sperm gets through, fertilization takes place and the zygote formed eventually develops into a new individual.

About Your Index

This index has been designed to help you find which articles will have information on the subject you are looking up. You may find that although there is no article on your subject, for example Aircraft, you will find a lot of information about it in other articles, such as Aerodynamics, Flight, Jet propulsion, and the Wright brothers.

The page numbers listed in this index are of different types. Those printed in **bold type** indicate where the main entry for the subject can be found, whereas page numbers in *italic type* refer to pages on which illustrations will be found. When you look up Acids and Bases, for example, you will see:

Acids and Bases 4, *4*
   litmus 347, 407
   pH 533, *533*

The main entry on this subject is on page 4 where there is also an illustration. Further information can be found under the articles on Litmus and pH.

After the main index you will find a Subject Index. In this all the articles in the encyclopedia are divided up by subject. The entries are in alphabetical order within each subject. In addition there is an index of entries which are Special Features.

Condensation **146**, *146*
Condenser *see* **Capacitor**
Condenser microphone 456
Conditioned reflex 394, 589
Conditioning, learning 394
Conduction, heat 147, *147*, 312, *312*
  thermal insulation 360
Conductors, electric 21, **147–148**, *147–148*
Cones, color vision 134, *234*
Conglomerates 613
Congreve, William 600
Conifers *79*, *127*
Conservation 148–149, *149*
  of energy 398
  momentum 468
Conservation, environmental 149, *149*
Constellation 150, *150*, 656
Construction 151, *151*
  cement 105
Contagious, definition 180
Continent 152, *152*
Continental drift *see* **Plate tectonics**
Contour lines 424
Contour maps *287*
Contraction 152–153, *152*, 312
Contrails *146*
Controller, automatic systems 48
Convection 147, **153**, *153*, 312, *312*
  thermal insulation 360
Converging lens *255*
Convex lens 396, *396*
Convex mirror *464*, 465
Cooke, William F. 690
Cooking, microwave ovens 458, *458*
Cooking oil *238*
Coordination 154, *154*
Copernicus, Nicolaus 154, *154–155*, 323, 381
Copper 155, *155*, *444*, *462*, 486
  alloys 21
  atoms *605*
  electric conductors *147*, 148
  melting point 438, *438*
  mining *463*
  specific heat capacity *650*
  trace element 708
Copper oxide *514*
Copper sulfate *112*, 209, *607*
Coral reef *218*, *503*
Cordierite hornfels *445*
Cordite 301
Coriolis force 107, 755
Corn *109*, 226, *329*
Cornea 233
Corneal grafting 711
Corning Glass Works 575
Corona 156, *156*, 193, 676
Corrosion 156, *156*
  anodizing metal 28
  electroplating 209
  stainless steel 654
Corticosterone 328
Cortisol 328
Cortisone 666
Corundum *308*
Cosmetics 157, *157*
Cosmic rays 157, *157*, *207*, 578–579

Cosmology 158
  see also **Universe**
Cosmonaut *see* **Astronaut**
Cotton 245, *245*, *531*
Cotton gin *349*
Cotyledon 158–159, *158–159*, 213, 614
Coulomb 159, *159*, 619
Coulomb, Charles-Augustin de 159
Coulter counter *359*
Counting:
  abacus 1, *1*
  numbers 497, 498–499, *498–499*
Courtelle 684
Courtship display 181
Cousteau, Jacques 32
Covalent bonds 77
Cow:
  breeding 82, *82*
  digestion 104, *666*
  milk 460
Cowpox *67*, 722
Crab, larvae 388
Crab Nebula *461*, 574
Cracking 160, *160*, 507
Cramer, Stuart 16
Crane, mechanical *574*
Crank 475
Crater, Moon 470, *470*
Crawford, Adair 669
Cretaceous Period 111, *227*, *232*, 288
Crevasses *292*
Crick, Francis 67, 69, 182, *182*, 325, 510, 763
Crickets, hearing 639
Crime, forensic science 262
Crippen, Robert 40
Crocodile 681
Crocodile bird 681
Crompton, Samuel *350*
Cronstedt, Axel Fredrik 486
Crookes, William 99, *99*, 100
Crookes tube 99
Cross-pollination 557
Crustaceans 126
  skeleton 622
Crux constellation 150
Cryogenics 131
Crystal microphone 456, *456*
Crystal Palace, London 96
Crystals 161, *161*
  atoms 634
  liquid crystals 407
  piezoelectricity 543, *543*
  rocks 602, *602*
  X-ray diffraction 762–763, *763*
Cube numbers 433
Cuckoo 357
Cullinan diamond 175
Cumulonimbus cloud *129*
Cumulus cloud *129*
Curie, Marie and Pierre 161–162, *162*, 324, 545, *545*, 582, 583
Current *see* **Electricity**
Cuttings, plants 329, *329*
Cuvier, Baron Georges 519, *519*
Cyclic accelerator 524–525, *524*
Cyclone 163, *163*, 332
Cyclosporine 712
Cyclotron *524*
Cygnus constellation 493

D

Dacron 684
Daguerre, Louis J.M. 165, 538
Daguerreotype 165, *165*, 537
Daimler, Gottlieb 363
Daisy *405*
Dalton, John 44, 45, *45*, 140, *212*, 324, 377, 540
Dams:
  hydroelectricity 336, *336*
  tidal power 699, *699–700*
Dark matter 431
Darwin, Charles 6, 67, **165–166**, *165–166*, 226, 322, 324, *385*, 479
Dating:
  carbon dating 93–94, *94*
  dendrochronology 170, *170*
  rocks 288
Davy, Humphry 166, *166*, 237, 324, 669
Daylength 167, *167*
DDT 530–531
De Forest, Lee 25, *25*
Dead Sea 225
Deadly nightshade *554*
Deafness 188
Decagon 560
Decibel 168, *168*
Deciduous trees 395
Decimal 62, **168**, *168*, 499
Deer 592
Deforestation 169, *169*
Dehydration 169–170, *170*, 331
Deimos 428, 609–610
Delta 598
Democritus 44, 114, 115, 322
Dendrochronology 170, *170*
Denier 502
Density 171, *171*
  specific gravity 649–650, *650*
Dentistry, amalgam *23*
Deoxyribonucleic acid *see* DNA
Depression 185, 572, 708
Depressions *see* **Cyclone**
Dermatitis 21
Dermatology 435
Desalination 171–172, *172*
Descartes, René 172, *172*
Desert 173, *173–174*, 386
  climate 133
  humidity 331–332
  hydroponics 341
  mirage 464, *464*
  oases *744*
Desertification 174, *174*
Detergent alcohols 19
Detergents *466*, **625–626**, *625–626*
  bubbles 83
  phosphates 534
  and surface tension 680, *680*
Detonators 231
Deuterium 315, *315*, 338, *338–339*, *373*, 493
Deuterons 553
Devonian Period *227*, *232*, 288
Devonian sandstone *613*
Dew 332, 564

Dewar, James 723, *724*
Dextrose 671
Diabetes 180, 284, 500
Dialysis, kidneys 381
Diamond 93, *93*, **175**, *175*
  hardness 307, *308*
  melting point *438*
Diaphragm:
  breathing *81*
  loudspeaker *411*
  microphone 456, *456*
Dickson, W.K.L. 537
Dicotyledon *79*, 127, *159*
Die, probability 569, *569*
Dielectric *see* **Insulators, electric**
Diesel, Rudolph 175, 217, 363
Diesel engine 175–176, *176*, 275, 362–363
Diet 500, *500–501*
  fats 237–238
  vitamins 737, *737*
Diffraction 176–177, *176–177*
  light 83, *83*
  waves 748, *748*
Diffusion 68, **177–178**, *177*
Digestion 178, *178*
  absorption 2
  enzymes 219, 294
  hydrochloric acid 336
  intestine 364, *364*
  liver 408, *408*
  pancreas 519–520, *520*
  protein 570
  stomach 666–667, *666*
Digital 179, *179*, 690
Digital Audio Tape (DAT) 641
Digital clocks and watches 128, *128*, 211
Digital code, laser disc 390
Digitalis 533
Digits, numbers 498, 499
Dimensions *see* **Measurement**
Dinorwic 337
Dinosaur:
  extinction 232
  fossils *264*, 519
Diode 179, *179*, 616
  definition 210
  Diode valve *724*, 725
Diorite 345
Dioscorides 533
Dirac, Paul 576
Direct current (DC) 202, *202*
  diode 179
  generators 283, *283*
  rectifier 586, *586*
Disabled, computer technology *653*
Disaccharides *671*, 672
Discovery (Space Shuttle) 648
Disease 180, *180*
  antibiotics 29
  antibodies and antigens 30, *30*, 346
  antiseptics 31–32
  cytology 164
  infection 351–352
  microbiology 453
  monoclonal antibodies 468–469
  parasites 523
  pathology 526, *526*
  vaccination 64, 67, 722, *722*

microchips 454
semiconductor 616, *616*
synthesizers 358
transistors 710, *710*
see also **Computer**
Electroplating 156, 204,
209, *209*
Electroscope, gold leaf 212,
212
Element, chemical
212–213, *212*
alchemy 18
analysis 26
atomic number 43, *43*
atoms 43
chemistry 114
compound 139–140, *140*
electrolysis 204, *204*
inorganic chemistry 356
isotopes 373
mass spectroscopy
429–430, *429*
molecules 467
periodic table 527–529
symbols 113, *113*
Elementary particles *see*
Subatomic particles
Elephant:
gestation 291, *291*
size 767
Elizabeth I, Queen of
England 157
Elk, Irish *226*
Ellipse *546*
Elliptical galaxy *276*
Embryo 213–214, *213*
in eggs 197
plant 158, 614
Empirical formula 263
Emulsion 131, **214**, *214*,
466, *466*
Enamel, teeth 687
Endangered species
214–215, *215*
Endocrine glands 294, *294*,
327
Endoparasites 523
Energy 216, *216*
from carbohydrate 92
conservation 149, *149*,
398
efficiency 196, 216
electricity 200, 202–203,
202–203
engines 217, *217*
entropy 218
explosives 231
flywheels 253–254
food 241–242, *501*
food chains 258
force 261
fuel 274, *274*
geothermal 216,
290–291, *291*
heat 311, *311*, 312
joule 377, *377*
Joule's law 377, *377*
kilowatt-hour 382, *382*
kinetic 216, *474*, *526*
latent heat 390–391, *391*
light 399–401, *400–401*
maser 428, *428*
metabolism 442
nuclear energy 216, 493,
493
nuclear reactor 495, *495*
potential 216, *526*
power 563, *563*
quantum mechanics 576
quantum theory 577, *577*
radiation 578–579, *578*

resources 594
solar 630–631, *630*
thermodynamics 697, *697*
tidal power 699–700,
699–700
work 760, *760*
see also **Power**
Engine 217, *217*
antifreeze 30–31
ceramic casings *108*
diesel 175–176, *176*
efficiency 196
flywheels 253–254
fuel injection 275, *275*
gas turbine 280–281, *280*
governor 297, *297*
heat exchangers 311
horsepower 328, *328*
internal combustion
engine 362–363, *363*,
689
ion propulsion 366, *366*
jet propulsion 374,
374–375
lubrication 411–412
steam 217, *253*, 659, *659*,
689, *760*
Wankel engine 741, *741*
English language 653
Entomology 766
Entropy 218
Environment 218–219, *218*
adaptation to 6
conservation 149, *149*
pollution 557–558,
558–559
Enzymes 98, **219–220**,
219–220
digestion 92, 178
feedback 240
glands 294
and metabolism 442, *442*
pancreas 519
Eocene period 344
Epoxy resin 7, **220–221**,
220, 548
Epsom salts 673
Equator 167, 316, *316*, 392
Equilateral triangle 560
Equus 226
Equilibrium 221–222, *221*
Eratosthenes 286
Erosion and Weathering
222–223, *222–223*
desertification 174
landforms 386, *387*
mountains 473, *473*
sedimentary rocks 613,
613
soil 169
Erythrocytes 75
Escape velocity 223–224,
224
Escarpment *387*
Escherichia coli 284
Esker *293*
Essential oils 505–506
Ester 561
Estuary *598*
Eta carinae nebula *461*
Etching *335*
Ethane 335, *335*, 569
Ethanediol 30, 267
Ethanol 19, 531–532, 764
Ethene 263, 531, 532, 561,
561
Ether 517
Ethoxyethane *see* Ether
Ethyl alcohol *see* Ethanol
Ethylene glycol 19, 30, 267
Ethylene *see* Ethene

Ethyne *see* Acetylene
Euclid 322, 432
Euglena *453*
Euler, Leonhard 323
Euphrates, River 424
Europa 378, *378*, 610
Europe
continent 152
early technology 688
size 286
European Space Agency
136
EVA suits *40*
Evaporation 224–225,
224–225
transpiration 711, *711*
Everest, Mount 43, 286,
472
Evergreen trees 395
Evolution 225–227,
226–227, 649
adaptation 6
Darwin's theory
165–166, *165–166*
fossils 518–519
Lamarck 384–385
mutation 183, *226*, 478
natural selection
479–480
Excretion 228, *228*
Exosphere *42*
Expansion 153, **229**, *229*,
312
Expansion theory 229, *229*
Experiment 230, *230*, *541*
chemistry *115*
laboratory 383–384, *383*
Explode, definition 61
Explosion
combustion 135
fireworks 248
Explosives 231, *231*
ammonia 24
gunpowder 301, *301*
nitric acid 487–488
nitroglycerine 488–490
TNT 704–705, *705*
External combustion
engine 217
Extinction 214–215, **232**,
232
Extractive metallurgy 444
Extrusion 233, *233*
Exxon Valdez 559
Eye *172*, **233–234**, *233–234*,
617, 618
binocular vision 63–64,
63
color vision 134, *134*
corneal grafts 711
in dreams 184
lenses 396
parallax 522, *522*
stereoscopic vision 64,
64, 664

F

Fabrics 430, *431*
natural fibers 245, *245*
synthetic fibers 502,
683–684, *684*
Facsimile transmission *see*
Fax
Factories *see* Industry
Fahrenheit 104–105, *105*,
235
Fahrenheit, Gabriel David
235
Fallout, radioactive
235–236, *235*

False-color photography
236, *236*
False oat grass *79*
Far East, early technology
688
Faraday, Michael 60, 202,
205, 206, **237**, *237*, 278,
282, 324, 348, 540
Farman, Henri 250
Farming *see* **Agriculture**
Far sight 234
Fast-breeder reactor 495
Fats 237–238, *237*
cholesterol 118
margarine 426
nutrition 500, *501*
thermal insulation 360
Fatty acids 238
Faults:
landforms 386, *386–387*
plate tectonics 550–551
Fax *137*, **238–239**, *239*
Fear, phobia 572
Feathers 239–240, *240*
pigments 544
thermal insulation 360
Feces 228, 364
Feedback 48, **240–241**, *241*
Feeding 241–242
Fermat 323
Fermentation 242–243, *242*
alcohol 19
yeast 764
Fermi, Enrico 484, *484*
Fermi National Accelerator
Laboratory 524, 525
Ferns 78
Fertilization 243, *244*, 591
cell division 102, *102*
egg 197
embryo 213, *213*
pollination 557
zygote 768, *768*
Fertilizers 244, *244*
ammonia *23*, 24
nitrates 487, *487*
phosphates 534
potassium 561
sulfur *673*
Fetus 214
Feynman, Richard 669, *669*
Fibonacci series *499*
Fiber:
cellulose 92, 104
in cereals 108
dietary 500
Fiber optics *see* **Optical**
fibers
Fibers, natural 245, *245*
Fibers, synthetic 683–684,
684
Filament, light bulb 399,
399, *714*
Film, photographic 87–88,
246, *246*, 537–538
cinematography
121–122, 537–538
Polaroid 555–556, *556*
Filoplumes 239
Filter, charcoal 111, *111*
Filter, electronic 247, *247*
Filter feeder 242
Filtrate 247
Filtration 247–248,
247–248
Fingerprint 262, *623*
Fire
burning 84, *84*
combustion 135, *135*
spontaneous combustion
653

I

Ice 229, *229*, 344, *344*
  dry ice 186, *186*
  dust particles *359*
  erosion *222*, 223
  freezing 267, 405, *745*
  glaciers *292–293*, 293
  hydrogen bonds 340
  precipitation 565
Ice Age 344, *344*
Icebergs *171*, 344, *344*, 637
Iceland, maps 425
Igneous rocks 345, *345*, 602, *602–603*
  formation 393
  metamorphic rocks 445–446
  mica 452
  ores 509
Ileum *see* **Intestine**
Illness *see* **Disease**
Immiscible, definition 466–467
Immune system 346, *346*
  AIDS 13
  antibiotics 29
  antibodies and antigens 30
  transplants 711–712
  vaccination 722, *722*
  viruses 735
Impeller 575
Impermeable, definition 37
Implode, definition 61
Implosion 346, *347*
Incidence, angle of 465
Incisor teeth 687, *687*
Inclined plane *416*
Incubators *435*
Index (mathematics) 433
India
  early technology 688
  monsoon 469
  music 477
  plastic surgery 547
Indian Ocean 503
monsoon 469, *469*
Indicator, chemical 347, *347*
  acids and bases 4
  litmus 407, **407**
  pH 533
  titration 704
Inductance, self and magnetic 348, *348*
Induction, electric
  generators 282–283
Induction coil 349, *349*
Industrial Revolution 130, **349–350**, *349–350*, 417, 596, 688, *689*, 715
Industry
  pollution 17, *17*, 558, 742
  robots 599
Inertia 350–351, *350–351*, 429
Inertial guidance 351, *351*, 465
Infection 180, **351–352**
  antiseptics 31–32
  definition 31
  immune system 346, *346*
  lymph system 414–415
Infectious, definition 180
Infinity 352, *352*, 498
Influenza 735
Information technology 353, *353*

Infrared astronomy 354, *354*
Infrared photography 354, *354*
Infrared radiation 206, *206*, **354–355**, *354*
  false-color photography 236
  spectrum 652
Inheritance *see* **Heredity**
Injection molding 355, *355*
Inoculation 722
Inorganic chemistry 356, *356*
  see also Chemistry Subject Index
Insecticide 226, 530–531, *673*
Insects
  antenna 28, *28*
  breathing 81
  camouflage 89, *89*
  ecosystem *195*
  hibernation 319
  larvae 388–389, *388*
  metamorphosis 446–447, *446–447*
  migration 459
  natural selection 480
  pigments 544
  pollination of flowers 557, *557*
  skeleton 622
Insoluble, definition 635
Instinct 58, **357**, *357*
Instruments, musical 357–358, *358*
  synthesizers 682–683, *683*
Instruments, scientific 359, *359*
Insulation
  foam rubber 255
  thermal 360, *360*
Insulators, electrical 148, 361, **361**, *361*
  alloys 21
  glass 294
Insulin
  diabetes 180
  functions 328, *520*
  genetic engineering 284, *284*
  pancreas 294, 520, *520*
Integrated circuit 210, *210–211*, **361**, *362*
  calculators 86
  computers 142, 145
  microchips 454, *454*
  microprocessors 456, *456*
Intel Corporation 456
Intelligence 362
  artificial 38, *38*
Interference, wave 176, *176*, 748
Internal combustion engine 217, **362–363**, *363*, 689
  diesel 175–176, *176*
  fuel injection 275, *275*
  gas turbine 280–281, *280*
  induction coil 349
  Wankel engine 741, *741*
International Council of Scientific Unions (ICSU) 604
Interstellar matter 364, *364*
Intestine 178, **364**, *364*
Inuit 6
Invention 365, *365*

Invertebrates 622
Involuntary muscles 476
Io 378, *378*, 610
Iodides 365
Iodine 365, *365*
  halogen lamps 306
  as indicator of starch 655, *655*
  metamorphosis of tadpoles 446
  radioisotopes 373
  as trace element 707–708
Ion 366, *366*
  bonds 77
  mass spectroscopy 429, 430
Ion propulsion 366, *366*
Ionization 366
Ionizing radiation 578, 763
Ionosphere 42, 190, **367**, *367*
  solar wind 631
  telecommunications 290, 579
Iridescence 367–368, *368*
Iridium 551
Iris *663*
Irish elk 226
Iron and Steel *115*, **368–369**, *369*, *444*
  alloys 21, 423–424
  blast furnaces 73–74, *73–74*
  cast iron 96
  in cereals 108
  expansion 229
  forging 262–263, *263*
  freezing point 268
  galvanizing 277–278
  melting point *438*
  rust (iron oxide) 156, *156*, 368, *513*, 514
  trace element 707–708
  valency 725
Iron chloride *635*
Irradiation 260, 261, **369–370**, *369–370*, 665
Irrigation *174*, 365, **370**, *370*
Iso, definition 371
Isobar 371, *371*
Isomer 371–372, *371*
Isometric, definition 371
Isosceles triangle 371, 560
Isotherm 372, *372*
Isotonic 372–373, *372*
  definition 371
Isotope 373, *373*, 484
  definition 371
  mass spectroscopy 429–430
  medical uses 583

J

Jacquard loom *350*
Japan
  paper-making *520*
  robots 599
Java, tsunamis 700–701
Jellyfish 742
Jenner, Edward 323, 722, *722*
Jensen, Johannes Hans 571, *571*
Jet propulsion 280, 374, *374–375*
Jet stream 375, *375*
Jetfoil 337
Jewelry, gold 296
Jews, medicine 435
Joint, universal *198*

Joints 376, *376*, 623
  artificial hips *695*
  lubrication 412
Joliot, Frederic 162
Joliot-Curie, Irene 162
Jolson, Al 122
Joule 216, 313, **377**, *377*, 382, 619
Joule, James Prescott 324, 377, *377*
Joule's law 377, *377*
Julian calendar 86
Juniper *405*
Juniperus communis 405
Jupiter 378, *378*, 632, *633*
  asteroids 39
  atmosphere 449
  escape velocity 224
  gravity 298
  moons 277, *277*, 609–610
  space probe 644, 645
Jurassic Period 227, *232*, *288*

K

Kalahari Desert 173
Kaleidoscope 379, *379*
Kangaroo *70*
Kaolin 562, *562*
Karst *603*
Keck telescope 693
Kekulé, August 60, 356
Kelly, Henry 368
Kelvin 380, *380*, 452, 619
Kelvin, William Thomson 377, **380**, *380*
Kelvin scale 105, *105*
Kennecott's Bingham Canyon mine *463*
Kennedy Space Center 646
Kepler, Johannes 41, 80, 158, 323, **380–381**, *380*
Keratin 239
Kerosene 335, 507
Kettle lakes *293*
Kevlar *430*
Keys and Locks 409, *409*
Khayyam, Omar 19
Kidneys 75, 228, *228*, **381**, *381*
Kilimanjaro, Mount 712
Kiln 382, *382*
Kilocalorie 377
Kilogram 452, 619, *619*
Kiloherz 318
Kilojoule 313, 377, 501
Kilowatt-hour 382, *382*
Kim's Game *439*
Kinetic energy 216, *474*, *526*
Kinetoscope *196*
Kipp's apparatus 356
Kirchhoff, Gustav Robert 148, *148*, 324, 545
Kirchhoff's laws 148
Klaproth, Martin 545
Knee joint 376, *376*
Knoll, Max 209
Koch, Robert 435, *435*, 453, 526
Kodak 537
Kokoi arrow-poison frog 554
Korea, paper-making *520*
Krakatoa 700–701, 738
Krypton 42, 402, 490–491
Kubasov, Valery 40

L

Labels, food 500
Laboratory *359*, **383–384**, *383–384*
Lactic acid 384, *384*, 593
Lactose 460, 672
Ladybug *65*
Lady's slipper orchid 215, 252
Lagoon nebula *461*
Lakes 597–598, *598*
Lamarck, Jean Baptiste 384–385, *384*
Laminated glass 295, 606
Laminates 385, *385*
 epoxy resins 221
 plastics *549*
Lamp, safety 166, *166*
Lamprey *241*
Land, Edwin 555
Land use maps *287*
Landforms 385–386, *386–387*
Langevin, Professor 637
Language translation by computers 388, *388*
Languages, computer 144, *144*
Lanner falcon *258*
Lanolin 118
Laplace, Marquis de 64
Large Magellanic Cloud 419, 481, 677, 678
Larva 388–389, *388*, 446–447, *446*
Larviparous *35*
Larynx 652, *652*
Laser 389–390, *389–390*
 bar code scanners 53
 compact disc players 138
 hologram 320–321, *321*
 navigation systems 139
 optical fibers 508
 rangefinders 584, *584*
 theodolites 696, *696*
Laser disc 390, *390*
Latent heat 313, **390–391**, *391*
Lateral line 188, 618
Latex 254, 604, *604–605*
Lathe 391, *391*, 416, 417
Latin names 405
Latitude and Longitude 392, *392*
 and daylength 167
 tropics 712–713, *713*
Laue, Max von 762
Lava 392–393, *392–393*, 738, *738*
 erosion 223
 igneous rocks 345
Lavoisier, Antoine 64, 114, *114*, 323, 515
Lawrencium 43, 527
Lead 393, *393*
 air pollution 17
 extrusion 233
 half-life *305*
 malleability *423*
 melting point *438*
 unleaded gasoline 505
Lead azide 231
Lead crystal 294
Lead oxide *514*
Leaf insect, camouflage *89*
Leap year 86–87, *702*
Learning 394, *394*
 intelligence 362
 learned behavior 58

Leather, tanning 685
Leaves *79*, **394–395**, *395*
 cotyledons 158–159, *158–159*, 213
 photosynthesis 539, *539*
 transpiration 711, *711*
Leclanché dry cell 56
Leeuwenhoek, Anton van 164, 455, 457, *457*
Leibnitz, Gottfried von 323, 432
Lens, optical 396, *396*
 camera 87, *88*, 537
 diffraction 177
 eyes 233–234, *234*
 focus 255
 magnification 422, *422*
 microscopes 208, 456–457
 refraction 589–590
 telescopes 692
Leonardo da Vinci 250, 322, 323, 397, *397*
Leonov, Alexei 40
Leopard *258*
Lesage, Georges 690
Lesser black-backed gull *649*
Letterpress 567
Leucocytes 75
Leukemia 711
Lever 33, 261–262, **397–398**, *397–398*, 416, *416*, 688
Leverrier, Urbain Jean Joseph 324, 482
Lewis Research Center 366
Leyden jar 398, *398*
Lichen
 litmus 347, 407
 symbiosis 681, *681*
Life expectancy 11, *11*
Life Sciences *see* Subject Index
Ligament 376, *376*
Light 399–401, *400–401*
 see also Physics Subject Index
 arc lamps 34, *34*
 bioluminescence 68, *68*
 chemical reactions 112
 color 134, *134*
 diffraction 83, *83*, 177
 Doppler effect 183, 184
 electric arc 199
 eyesight 233–234, *234*
 focusing 255
 frequency 268
 iridescence 367–368
 laser 389–390, *389–390*
 luminescence 412–413, *412*
 mirage 464, *464*
 mirrors 464–465, *464–465*
 optical lenses 396, *396*
 photochemistry 535, *535*
 photoelectric cells 536–537, *536*
 photosynthesis 539, *539*
 polarized 555, *555*
 prisms 568, *568*
 quantum mechanics 576
 quantum theory 577, *577*
 rainbows 583, *583*
 red shift 229, 587–588, *587*
 reflection 588, *588*
 refraction 589–590, *589*
 solar cells 629, *629*
 spectroscopy 651, *651*

 spectrum 651–652, *652*
 speed of 400, 401, 404
 stroboscopes 668–669
 ultraviolet 134, 718–719, *718–719*
 velocity 729
 visible light 207, *400*
 wavelength 206–207
Light bulb 399, *399*
 filaments 714, *714*
 gases 402
 heat 313
 invention of 196, *196*
 power 563, *563*
Light-emitting diodes (LED) *86*
Light meter 399, *399*
Light pen *143*
Light-year 404, *404*, 523
Lighting, artificial 402, *402*
 neon 481, *481*
Lightning 202, **403**, *403*
 Franklin's experiment 266, *266*
 thunder 699, *699*
Lightning rod 266, *266*, **403**, *403*
Lignin 758–759
Limestone 85, 288, 602–603
 formation of 613, *613*
 karst *603*
 marble 446, *446*
 stalactites and stalagmites 654–655, *654–655*
 weathering 223
Limpet *623*
Line graph 297, *297*
Linear accelerator (linac) 524–525, *524*
Linear motor 404, *404*, 420
Linen 245
Linnaeus, Carolus 67, 78, 125, 323, **405**, *405*
Lion *241*, *258*
Lipids 237, 505
Lipoproteins 118
Lippershey, Hans 41, 692
Liquefied petroleum gas (LPG) 569–570
Liquid 405–406, *406*, 431, 657
 absorption 2
 boiling point 76, *76*
 Brownian motion 82
 buoyancy 84, *84*
 capillary action 91, *91*
 condensation 146, *146*
 convection 153
 density 171, *171*
 diffusion 177
 distillation 181–182
 emulsion 214, *214*
 evaporation 224–225, *224–225*
 filtration 247
 flash point 249
 fluids 253
 freezing 267, 268
 hydrometers 340, *340*
 melting point 438, *438*
 meniscus 439–440, *439–440*
 osmosis 513, *513*
 siphon 621, *621*
 solution 635, *635*
 solvent 636, *636*
 specific gravity 650, *650*
 surface tension 679–680, *679–680*

 suspension 680–681, *680*
 viscosity 736, *736*
Liquid column chromatography 118–119
Liquid crystal display (LCD) 406, *406–407*, 601, 736
Liquid crystals 406, **407**
Lister, Joseph 31, *31*, 32, 324
Listeria 260
Lithium battery 56
Lithography 567–568
Lithosphere 190
Litmus 4, 347, *347*, **407**, *407*
Liver 178, **408**, *408*
 cholesterol production 118
Liverpool-Manchester Railway 659
Lizards
 body temperature *312*
 ears 188
 symmetry *682*
Lobster *623*
Locks and Keys 409, *409*
Locomotion *see* **Movement and Motion**
Locust *226*, *258*, 459
Lodge, Oliver Joseph 206, *206*
Logarithms *432*
Logic 410, *410*
Logo computer language 144
Longitude *see* **Latitude and Longitude**
Loom, Jacquard *350*
Lorentz, Hendrik Antoon 588, *588*
Loudspeaker 411, *411*, 641
 electromagnets 205
 hi-fi 320
 stereophonic sound 663, *663*
Lovell, Bernard 580–581
Low explosives 231
Lowell, Percival 552, *552*
Lubrication 270, **411–412**, *411–412*
Luciferin 68
Lucretius 453
Lumière brothers 122, 537–538
Luminescence 68, **412–413**, *412*
Luna space probe 644
Lunar eclipse 192–193, *193*
Lunar geology 288
Lungs 413–414, *413*
 blood circulation 124
 breathing 81, *81*, 593, *593*
 disease 17, 39
Luteinizing hormone (LH) *327*
Lyell, Charles 288, *288*, 324
Lymph system 414–415, *415*
Lymphocytes *415*

M

McCandless, Bruce 40
McClintock, Barbara 285, *285*
Mach, Ernst 417, *417*
Mach number 417, *417*, 638
Machine tools 416–417, *417*

Plinius 393
Pliohippus 226
Plow constellation *656*
Pluto 441, **551–552**, *552*,
632, *633*
    escape velocity 224
    gravity 298
    moon 609
    orbit 482
    space probe 642
Plutonium 553, *553*
    nuclear reactors 274, 495
    production from uranium
    720
    radioisotopes *583*
Plywood 385
Pneumatics 553–554, *553*
Poisoning, food 260, *260*
Poisons 554, *554*
    arsenic 36–37
    definition 554
    pesticides 530–531
Polar bear 6, 215, *304, 709*
Polar climate 133
Polaris *564*
Polarized light 555, *555*
Polaroid camera 88, 537,
555–556, *555–556*
Pole Star *564*
Poles 556, *556*
Police, forensic science 262
Polio 735
Pollen and Pollination 243,
252, **557**, *557*
    allergies to 20
Pollution 557–558, *558–559*
    acid rain 3, *3*
    air 14, 17, *17*, 256, 558,
    558–559, 674
    damage to ozone layer
    10, 117, 516
    environmental 219
    fertilizers 244, *244*
    greenhouse effect
    298–299, *299*
    lead 393
    nitrates 487
    noise 5
    ozone 516
    phates 534
    water 558, *558*, 742–743,
    743
Polonium 162, *305, 339*
Polyacrylic 684
Polyamide 561, 684
Polychloroethene 561
Polyester *531*, 561, 684
Polyethene 561
Polyethylene *see*
    Polyethene
Polygon 560, *560*
    symmetry 682
    tessellation *432*
Polymer *115*, **560–561**, *561*
    and desalination 172
    nylon 502
    plastics 548
    synthetic fibers 684
Polyphenylethene 561
Polytetrafluoroethene 561
Polythene *531, 531*, 532,
548, 561, *561*
Polyunsaturated fats 238
Polyurethane *531*
Polyvinyl chloride (PVC)
548, 561
Pompeii 322, 739
Population
    maps *287*
    world *286*
Porcelain 562, *562*

Porous, definition 37
Positive feedback 241
Positron 31, **561**, 669
Potash 561
Potassium 561–562, *562*
    fertilizers 244
    trace element 707–708
Potassium bromide 561
Potassium carbonate
    (potash) 561
Potassium chloride 561
Potassium dichromate *562*
Potassium fluoride 608
Potassium hydroxide 341,
341, 562
Potassium nitrate
    (saltpeter) 257, 301, 487,
561
Potassium permanganate
424
Potato *591*, 663
Potato prints *567*
Potential difference 739
Potential energy 216, *526*
Pottery and Porcelain 108,
562, *562*
    kilns 382, *382*
Power 563, *563*
    horsepower 328, *328*
    hydraulics 334–335
    solar power 630–631, *630*
    watt 747
    wave power 749–750,
    749
    wind power 756–757,
    756–757
    see also **Energy**
Power stations
    dynamos 348
    efficiency 196
    electricity *203*
    fuel 274
    hydroelectricity 336–337,
    336
    nuclear reactors 495, *495*
    tidal 699–700, *699–700*
Pre-Cambrian era *227, 232*,
288, 344, 518
Precession 302, *302*, **564**,
564
Precipitate 564
Precipitation 564–565, *565*
    see also Rain
Predator 258
Preece, William 425
Pregnancy *460, 718*
Premolar teeth 687, *687*
Preservation, food *see* **Food**
    preservation
Pressure 566, *566*
    air 14, *14*, 76
    atmospheric 42, 55
    gas 279–280, *279*
    implosion 346
    Magdeburg spheres 418,
    418
    osmotic 342
    water 33, 745
Priestley, Joseph 115, 515,
515
Primary cells, batteries 56
Primary colors *134*
Primary explosives 231
Prime numbers 498
Printed circuit *see*
    Electronics
Printing 567–568, *567, 688*
    etching *335*
Prism *134*, **568**, *568*
Probability 568–569,
568–569, 660

Progesterone 328
Program, computer 141,
144
Projectile, definition 52
Projection, map 425, *425*
Prolactin 328
Prominences, Sun 675, 676
Propane 140, 335, 479,
569–570, *569–570*
Propanetriol *see* **Glycerol**
Propanone 70, 531
Propellants, aerosols 10
Propylene 296
Protactinium *305*
Protein 335, **570**, *570*
    in cereals 108
    hydrogen bonds 340
    liver function 408
    in living cells 121
    molecules 510, 561
    nutrition 500, *501*
Proton 43, *43*, 44, 45, 207,
208, **570–571**, *571*,
669–670
    cosmic rays 157
    mass number 429, *429*
    nuclear physics 494
Protozoa 126, 455
Proxima Centauri 404, **571**,
571, 656
Psittacosis 732
Psychiatry 572, *572*
Psychoanalysis 269
Psychology and Psychiatry
362, **572**, *572*
Psychrometer 342, *342*
Pteridines 544
Pteridophytes 127, *232*
PTFE 561
Ptolemy 150, 286, *86*, 322,
425, **573**, *573*
Public opinion poll 660
Puffball fungus *591*
Pulley 33, 416, *416*, 434,
573–574, *573–574, 688*
Pulsar 485, **574**, *574*, 762
Pulse *310*
Pulse laser 389
Pumice 1, 392–393, *603*
Pump 575, *575*
Punch card *353*
Pupa 388, *446*, 447
Pupil, eye 233–234, *234*
PVC 548, 561
Pylon 151
Pyramids, Egypt 432, *433*
Pyrethrum 530
Pyrex 575, *575*
Pyrolusite 423
Pyrrhotite 486
Pythagoras 289
Pythagorean Theorem 289,
289

Q

Quadraphonic sound 664
Qualitative analysis 26
Quantitative analysis 26
Quantum mechanics 148,
434, 545, **576–577**,
Quantum theory 198, **577**,
577
Quark 44, 494, 670
    Gell-Mann 325
Quarrying *463*
Quartz *462*
    abrasives 1
    clocks and watches *128*,
    702, *702*

    hardness *308*
    piezoelectricity 543, *543*
Quartzite 223, 446
Quasar 577, *577*, 588, 762
Quaternary Period *232*
Quebec, meteorite 448
Quicksilver *see* **Mercury**
Quinine 533

R

Rabbit
    babies *70*
    digestion 104
    teeth 687
Rabies 732, 735
Radar *206*, **578**, *578*
Radial symmetry *682*
Radiation 147, **578–579**,
578
    cosmic rays 157, *157*
    electromagnetic
    206–207, *206–207*
    from Sun 43
    heat 312, *312*
    infrared 206, 236,
    354–355, *354*
    irradiation 369–370,
    369–370
    and mutation 478
    spectroscopy 651
    thermal insulation 360
    ultraviolet *207*
Radiation sickness 578
Radiation therapy 89
Radiator, heating system
311, 315
Radio 579–580, *579–581*,
690
    antenna 28–29, *28*
    cellular 103, *103*
    loudspeakers 411
    Marconi's invention
    425–426
    tuners 320
    see also Radio waves
Radio astronomy 577,
580–581, *580*
Radio telescope *41*,
580–581, **581–582**
Radio waves 206, *207*, 652
    frequency 268, 318
    ionosphere 367
    metal detectors 442–443,
    443
    reflection 588
    television 50–51
    ultra high frequency
    (UHF) 717
    very high frequency
    (VHF) 731, *731*
Radioactivity 582, *582*
    dating *288*
    fallout 235–236, *235*
    gamma rays 207
    Geiger counters 282, *282*
    half-life 305, *305*, 582,
    583
    Marie and Pierre Curie
    161–162, *162*
    nuclear waste 496
    pitchblende 545
    plutonium 553
    subatomic particles 669
Radioisotope 582–583, *583*
    half-life 305, 373
    iodine 365
    uses 373, *373*
Radium 162, *305*, 545, *545*,
583

thunder 699, *699*
ultrasound 717–718, *718*
Sound barrier 417, **640**, *640*, 678
Sound recording 640–641, *641*
  magnetic tape 420, *420*, 685–686, *685*, 734, *734*
Souter Point lighthouse 34
South Africa, gold 296
South America
  continent 152
  mountains *473*
South Pole 316, *316*, 556, *556*
  changing position of 152
  magnetic pole 289, *289*
  meridians 392
  ozone layer 516
  troposphere 714
  weather observations *450*
  see also Antarctica
Southern Cross
  constellation 150
Southern Hemisphere 316, *316*
Soviet Union
  Caspian Sea 286
  gold 296
  hydrogen bombs 338
  natural gas 479
  oil reserves 532
  space exploration 642, 647, *647*
Space exploration 641–642, *642–643*
  see also Astronomy
    Subject Index
  astronauts 40, *40*
  escape velocity 223–224, *224*
  heat exchangers 311
  heat shields 314, *314*
  ion propulsion 366, *366*
  satellites 608–609, *608*
  thermal insulation 360
Space medicine 644, *644*
Space probes 25, 553, 642, *642*, **644–645**, *645*
Space Shuttle 135, 314, *314*, 627, 642, 643, 644, **646**, *646*, 648
Space stations 646–647, *647*
Space telescope 647–648, *648*
Space-time 648, *648*, 702
Spacecraft *see* **Space exploration**
Spacelab 646
Spark plug *361*
Spaying 665
Speciation 226
Species 125, **649**, *649*
  reproduction 591
  symbiosis 681, *681*
Specific gravity 649–650, *650*
Specific heat capacity 650–651, *650*
Spectacles 234, *234*
Spectrometry, definition 26
Spectroscopy 651, *651*
  mass spectroscopy 429–430, *429*
Spectrum *400*, **651–652**, *652*
  prism 568, *568*
Speech 652, *652*
Speech recognition 653, *653*
Speed 474, *474*
  acceleration 2–3, *2*

Mach number 417, *417*
  of sound 638, 639
  velocity 729, *729*
Sperm *213*, 243, *243*, 768, *768*
Spermatophyta 127
Sphenodon 234
Spiders
  instinct 357
  poisons 554
  skeleton 622
  webs 767
Spine
  joints 376
  vertebrae 623
Spinning jenny *349*
Spinning mule *350*
Spiral galaxy *276*
Spirogyra 78
Spittler 510
Spleen *415*
Spontaneous combustion 135, **653**
Spontaneous generation, Aristotle's theory *35*
Spores *78*
Spring balances 612, *612*
Spring tides 701, *701*
Springs *299*
Sputnik 1 608, 641, 642
Square, definition 560
Square number 433, *499*
Squid *374*, 766
Squirrel 319
Stabilizers
  in foams 254
  gyrostabilizers 303, *303*
Stable equilibrium 221, 222
Stafford, Thomas 40
Stainless steel 369, **654**, *654*
  chromium content 120
  manganese content 424
Stalactites and Stalagmites 654–655, *654–655*
Stamen 252, 557, *557*
Stanford Linear Collider 110
Staphylococcus 260
"Star of Africa" diamond 175
Starch 655, *655*
  adhesives 7
  carbohydrate 92
  cereals 108
  digestion 178
Starfish *682*
  larvae 388, *388*
Stars 41, **656**, *656*
  see also Astronomy
    Subject Index
  binary stars 63, *63*, 728, *728*
  black holes 72–73, *72*
  constellations 150, *150*, 656
  galaxies 276, *276*
  globular clusters 295, *295*
  implosion 346
  infrared astronomy 354
  Milky Way galaxy 460–461, *461*
  nebulae 480–481
  neutron stars 485, *485*
  novae 492–493, *492*
  parallax 522, 523
  planetariums 546–547, *546*
  planets 546, *546*
  Proxima Centauri 571, *571*
  pulsars 574, *574*

radio astronomy 580–581, *580*
  red giants 587, *587*, 754
  Sirius 621–622, *621*
  supernovae 677–678, *677–679*
  variable stars 728–729, *728*
  white dwarfs 754, *754*
  X-ray astronomy 762, *762*
States of matter 657, *657*
Static electricity 212, **657–658**, *657*, 699
Statistics 48–49, *433*, **658**, **660–661**, *660–661*
  see also Mathematics
    Subject Index
Steady State theory 158
Steam 76, **658**, *658*
  condensation 146, *146*
  geothermal energy 290, *291*
Steam engine 217, **659**, *659*, 689
  flywheel *253*
  governor 297
  Hero's turbine 318, *318*
  Industrial Revolution 349, 350
  steam turbine 716, *716*
  work *760*
Steel 21, **368–369**, *369*
  forging 262
  galvanizing 277–278, *278*, 765
  manganese alloys *423*, 424
  rusting *513*
  stainless 120, 424, 654, *654*
  tempering 695
Stem 662–663, *662–663*
Step-down transformer *709*, 710
Step-up transformer *709*, 710
Stephenson, George 659
Stereophonic sound 320, **663–664**, *663*
  loudspeakers 411
  records 542–543, 585
Stereoscope 664, *664*
Stereoscopic photography 664
Stereoscopic vision 64, *64*
Sterilization 665, *665*
Steroids 665–666
Stevinus, Simon 323
Stibnite *462*
Stigma 252, 557, *557*
Still, distillation 181
Stimulants 708–709
"Stitch" (muscle pain) 384
Stockton-Darlington Railway 659
Stomach 178, **666–667**, *666*
Stomata 395, 711
Stone Age
  axes *431*
  cave paintings 518
Stonehenge 541
Stopping distance 729
Stores, laser tills 390
Storms
  cyclones 163, *163*
  hurricanes 332, *332*
  lightning 403, *403*
  thunder 699, *699*
  tornado 705–706, *705–706*

Stove, Franklin 266
Strassman, Fritz 494
Stratigraphy 288
Stratocumulus cloud *129*
Stratosphere 42, 190, **667**, *667*, 714
Stratus cloud *129*
Strawberry plant *82*
Streamlining 9, **667–668**, *667–668*, 736
Streams, environment 218–219
Stress, metal fatigue 443, *443*, *444*
Stress hormones 327
Stringed instruments 358, 477
Strip lighting 399, *402*
Strip mine 463
Stroboscope 668–669, *668*
Strong force 494
Strontium *444*, **669**
Strontium-90 *235*, 583
Structural formula 263
Styrene *see* Phenylethene
Styrofoam 561
Subarctic climate 133
Subatomic particles 669–670, *669*
  antimatter 31
  electrons 207–208, *208*
  elements 213
  neutrons 484
  positrons 561
  protons 570–571, *571*
  quantum mechanics 576–577
  radioactivity 582
Sublimation 634
Submarine 670–671, *670–671*
  sonar 637
  specific gravity 650
Subsoil *628*
Subsonic speed 417
Sucrose 672
Sugar beet 672
Sugar cane *672*
Sugars 92, **671–672**, *671–672*
  as a compound 140
  digestion 178
Sulfa drugs 672
Sulfates 672–673, *673*, 675
Sulfides 673, *673*
Sulfonamides 672
Sulfur 115, *462*, **673–674**, *673–674*, 708
Sulfur dioxide 674, *674*
  air pollution 14, 17, 558
Sulfur trioxide 514
Sulfuric acid 514, **674–675**, *674–675*
  batteries 56
  bleaching with 74
  sulfates 672
  uses 4
Sumerians, physics 541
Sun 41, 656, **675–676**, *675–676*
  asteroids 39, *39*
  and auroras 46
  and climate 132–133
  Copernicus's theory 154, *155*
  corona 156, *156*, 193
  daylength 167, *167*
  Earth's revolutions around 34–35
  eclipse 192–193, *193*
  energy 216, *216*

leaves 395
lifespan *11*
pollen and pollination 557
seeds 614
trunks 662
wood 758–759, *758*
Triangle 560
Triassic Period 227, *232*, *288*
Triceps muscle *476*
Triffid nebula *461*
Trilobite 232
Trinitrophenol *see* Picric acid
Triode tube *724*, 725
Triskaidekaphobia 572
Tristan da Cunha 393
Tritium 338, *338–339*, *373*
Triton *482*, 483, 609
Tropical rain forest *see* Rain forest
Tropical rainy climate 133
Tropics 712–713, *713*
Tropopause 714
Troposphere *42*, 190, **714**, *714*
Trumpet *477*
Trypsin 219
Tsetse fly *65*
Tsunamis 700–701, *700*
Tuatara 234
Tube, vacuum 724–725 *724–725*
Tuberculosis 525, 722, 732
Tuber *663*
Tufa 223
Tumor, definition 89
Tungsten 634, **714–715**, *714*
Tungsten carbide *714*, 715
Tuning fork *638*
Tunnel 715, *715*
Tupolev aircraft 678–679
Turbine 716, *716*
gas 217, 280–281, *280*, *362–33*, 374, *374–375*
hydroelectricity 336
Turbofan 374, *375*
Turbojet 374, *375*
Turboprop 280, 374, *375*
Turboshaft 280–281, 374
Turtle, computer *143*, 144
Turtle (submarine) 670
Twilight 713
Twins 128–129
Typemetal 703

U

U-boats 671
Ultrahigh frequency (UHF) 717, *717*
Ultrasound 637, **717–718**, *718*
Ultraviolet radiation *207*, **718–719**, *718–719*
fluorescent lighting 402, *402*
insects' eyes 134
ozone layer 43, 516
spectrum 652
Ulysses space probe 644
Umbriel 609
Uncertainty principle 576–577
Understanding, intelligence 362
United States of America
hydrogen bombs 338
natural gas 479

oil reserves 532
space exploration 642, 646, 647
Universal indicator *347*
Universal joint *198*
Universe 719–720, *719*
Big Bang theory 60, *60*
Big Crunch theory 60, *61*
Copernicus's theory 154
cosmology 158
entropy 218
expansion theory 229, *229*
galaxies 276, *276*
interstellar matter 364, *364*
matter 431
Ptolemaic system 573, *573*
see also **Planets; Solar System; Stars**
Unsaturated fats 238, *238*
Unstable equilibrium *221*, 222
Uraninite 545
Uranium 529, **720**, *720*
half-life *305*
hydrogen bombs 338, *338–339*
mass number 429
nuclear fission *493*
nuclear reactors 274, 495
pitchblende 545
plutonium 553
radium 583
Uranus 632, *633*, **721**, *721*
atmosphere 449
escape velocity 224
gravity 298
moons 609
orbit 482
Urea 228, 381, 408
Urethane foam 548
Urinary system 228, *228*
Urine 228, *228*, 381
Ursa Major constellation 150
USSR *see* Soviet Union
Utah *613*
Utah National Park *223*

V

Vaccination 64, 67, 180, 346, **722**, *722*
Vacuum 723, *723*
Magdeburg spheres 418, *418*
thermal insulation 360
Vacuum cleaner 723, *723*
Vacuum bottle 723–724, *724*
Vacuum forming, plastics *549*
Vacuum tube 724–725, *724–725*
Valency 725, *725*
Valles Marineris 427, *427*
Valley, landform 386, *386–387*
Valve 724–725, *724–725*
Van Allen, James 726
Van Allen belts *47*, **725–726**, *726*
Van de Graaff, Robert Jemison 726
Van de Graaff generator 726–727, *726–727*
Vandenberg Air Force Base, California 646

Vapor 727–728, *727–728*
boiling point 76, *76*
clouds 129–130, *129*
condensation 146, *146*
distillation 181
evaporation 225
flash point 249
fog 256
humidity 331
liquefying 406
steam 658, *658*
Variable stars 728–729, *728*
Vega (star) *564*
Vegetable oil 505
margarine 426, *426*
Vegetables 272
horticulture 329
hydroponics 341
Vegetarian diet 500
Vegetative reproduction 591–592, *591*
Vehicles
air pollution 17
brakes *270*
catalytic converters 98–99, *99*
electric 200, *200*
hovercraft 330, *330–331*
pollution 558, *558*
stopping distances 729
streamlining 668
wheels *541*
Vein 124, *124*
Velcro fastener *502*
Velocity 474, **729**, *729*
escape 223–224, *224*
momentum 468
terminal 695, *695*
see also Speed
Venera space probe *642*, 645
Venom, definition 554
Venus 609, 632, *633*, **730**, *730*
atmosphere 94
escape velocity 224
gravity 298
space probes 642, *642*, 644, 645
Verrocchio, Andrea del 397
Vertebra 376, 623
Vertebrates
breathing 81
evolution 227
skeleton 77, 622, *622*
see also Animals
Very high frequency (VHF) 731, *731*
Vesalius, Andreas 323, 476, *476*
Vesuvius, Mount 322, 739
Veterinary medicine 732, *732*
see also Life Sciences Subject Index
Vibration, music 477
Video camera 733, *733*
Videodisc 390
Videocassette recorder 308–309, **734**, *734*
Video tape 420, *420*, 686
Viking space probe 427, *428*, 642, 645, *645*
Vinegar *4*, 313, 634–635
Vinyl *531*
Vinyl chloride *see* Chloroethene
Violin 309, 358, *358*, 477
Virchow, Rudolph 526
Viruses and Viral diseases

29, 180, 455, *511*, **735**, *735*
AIDS 13, *13*
antibodies 346
antigens 30
biotechnology 70
infection 351–352
microbiology 453
Viscose 104, *684*
Viscosity 736, *736*
Visible light *207*
white light *400*
Vision 233–234, *233–234*, 617–618, *617*
binocular 63–64, *63*, 664
color vision 134, *134*
Descartes' theory *172*
parallax 522, *522*
stereoscopic 64, *64*
Visual display unit (VDU) 736, *736*
Vitamins 500, *501*, **737**, *737*
in cereals 108
food additives 256
Vivianite 535
Viviparous animals *35*
Vocal cords 652, *652*
Voice 492
Voice print 653
Volatile, definition 225
Volcanoes 738–739, *738–739*
lava 392–393, *393*
mountain building 473, *473*
plate tectonics *551*
tsunamis 700–701, *700*
Volt 619, **739–740**, *740*
Volta, Alessandro 202, *202*, 278, 324, 740
Voltmeter 739–740, *740*
Volume, measurement 436
Voluntary muscles 476
Voluntary nervous system 484
Voyager (aircraft) 250
Voyager space probe 25, *236*, 483, 553, *642*, 644, 645, *645*, 721
Vulcanizing 255, **740**, *740*
Vulture *258*

W

Wales, hydroelectricity 337
Wallace, Alfred 226
Walton, Ernest 524, *524*, 540
Wankel, Felix 741
Wankel engine 741, *741*
Warm-blooded animals *312*
Warm front 271, *271*
Wasp 326
Waste disposal 741–742, *742–743*, 558
excretion 228, *228*
Watches 128, *128*, 702, *702*
digital *211*
quartz 543, *543*
Water 405, **742**, **744–745**, *744–745*
Archimedean screw 33, *33*
artesian wells 37, *37*
boiling point *76*
clouds 129–130, *129*
dehydration 169–170, *170*
desalination 171–172

Subject Index

Astronomy

Biographies

Chemistry

Earth Science

Map projections
Metamorphic rocks
Meteorology
Mica
Minerals
Mining
Monsoon
Mountains
Natural gas
Nuclear waste
Ocean
Oils
Ore
Ozone layer
Plate tectonics
Poles
Pollution
Precipitation
Rainbow
Recycling
Resonance
Resources
Richter scale
Rivers and Lakes
Rocks
Sedimentary rocks
Seismograph
Soil
Stalactites and
  Stalagmites
Stratosphere
Theodolite
Thunder
Tidal power
Tidal waves and
  Tsunamis
Tides
Tornado
Tropics
Troposphere
Van Allen belts
Volcanoes
Waste disposal
Water
Water pollution
Water supply
Water table
Weather
Wind
Wind power

Electronics

Bar code
Bit and Byte
Calculator
Capacitor
Computer
Computer graphics
Computer languages
Computer memory
Digital
Diode
Electronics
Feedback
Filter, electronic
Hardware
Information technology
Integrated circuit
Language translation by
  computers
Logic
Microchip
Microprocessor
Modem
Rectifier
Robots
Semiconductor
Software
Speech recognition
Synthesizer
Transistor
Vacuum tube

Visual display unit
  (VDU)
Word processor

Life Science

Adaptation
Adolescence
Aging
Agriculture
AIDS
Allergy
Anatomy
Antenna
Antibiotics
Antibodies and Antigens
Antiseptics
Behavior
Binocular vision
Biochemistry
Biological control
Biology
Bioluminescence
Biophysics
Biotechnology
Birth
Blood
Bone
Botany
Brain
Breathing
Breeding
Camouflage
Cancer
Carbohydrate
Carbon dioxide
Cell
Cell division
Cellulose
Cereals
Chlorophyll
Cholesterol
Chromosomes and
  Genes
Circulation
Classification
Clones
Conservation,
  environmental
Coordination
Cotyledon
Cytology
Dehydration
Dendrochronology
Digestion
Disease
Display
DNA
Dreams
Drug
Ear
Ecology
Ecosystem
Egg
Embryo
Endangered species
Environment
Enzymes
Evolution
Excretion
Experiment
Extinction
Eye
Fats
Feathers
Feedback
Feeding
Fermentation
Fertilization
Fertilizers
Fibers
Flowers
Food chain

Food poisoning
Forensic science
Fruit
Genetic engineering
Genetics
Gestation
Gills
Glands
Growth
Hair
Heart
Heredity
Hibernation
Homing
Hormone
Horticulture
Hybrid
Hydroponics
Hypothermia
Immune system
Infection
Instinct
Intelligence
Intestine
Joints
Kidneys
Laboratory
Lactic acid
Larva
Learning
Leaves
Liver
Lungs
Lymph system
Medicine
Memory
Metabolism
Metamorphosis
Microbiology
Microorganism
Migration
Milk
Monoclonal antibody
Movement and Motion
Muscle
Mutation
Natural selection
Nerves
Nicotine
Nose
Nucleic acid
Nucleus, cell
Nutrition
Oils
Organism
Osmosis
Pain
Paleontology
Pancreas
Parasite
Pasteurizaton
Pathology
Pesticides
Pharmacology
Photosynthesis
Physiology
Pigments
Plastic surgery
Poisons
Pollen and Pollination
Protein
Psychology and
  Psychiatry
Reflex
Reproduction
Respiration
Roots
Rubber
Seeds
Semipermeable
  membrane
Senses
SI Units

Skeleton
Skin
Sleep
Soil
Space medicine
Species
Speech
Starch
Stem
Sterilization
Steroids
Stomach
Streamlining
Sugars
Sulfa drugs
Symbiosis
Tannin
Taste
Teeth
Touch
Tranquillizers and
  Stimulants
Transpiration
Transplants
Vaccination
Veterinary medicine
Virus and Viral diseases
Vitamins
Water
Water supply
Wax
Wood
Yeast
Zoology
Zygote

Mathematics √

Abacus
Algebra
Arithmetic
Average
Binary numbers
Decimal
Geometry
Graph
Infinity
Latitude and Longitude
Light year
Logic
Map
Map projections
Mass
Mathematics
Measurement
Metric system
Numbers
Optical character
  recognition
Oscillator
Polygon
Probability
Ratio
Rotation
Scales and Balances
Statistics
Symmetry
Weights and Measures

Physics

Absorption
Acceleration
Acoustics
Aerodynamics
Aerosol
Ampere
Antimatter
Atomic number
Atomic weight
Balancing point
Ballistics
Battery

Bimetallic strip
Bioluminescence
Biophysics
Black body
Boiling point
Brownian motion
Bubbles
Buoyancy
Capacitor
Capillary action
Carbon dating
Cathode-ray tube
Celsius
Center of gravity
Centrifugal force
Circuit, breaker
Circuit, electric
Cold
Color
Compass
Condensation
Conduction, heat
Conductors, electric
Conservation
Contraction
Convection
Coulomb
Decibel
Density
Diffraction
Doppler effect
Echo
Efficiency
Elasticity
Electric arc
Electricity
Electromagnet
Electromagnetic radiation
Energy
Entropy
Equilibrium
Escape velocity
Expansion
Experiment
Fahrenheit
Fallout, radioactive
Filter, electronic
Flotation
Fluid
Focus
Force
Foucault pendulum
Frequency
Friction
Fuse
Galvanometer
Gas
Generator, electric
Gravity
Gyrocompass
Gyroscope
Half-life
Hardness
Harmonics
Heat
Hertz
Hologram
Horsepower
Hydroelectricity
Hydrogen bomb
Hydrometer
Hygrometer
Implosion
Inductance, self and
  magnetic
Induction coil
Inertia
Inertial guidance
Infrared radiation
Insulation, thermal
Insulators, electrical
Iridescence
Joule

Technology

Special Features Index

Energy
Evolution
Experiment
Flight
Flowers
Food chain
Fruit
Genetics
Geography
Geology

Heat
History of Science
Horticulture
Inorganic chemistry
Instruments, scientific
Landforms
Light
Magnetism
Mathematics
Measurement

Medicine
Meteorology
Microbiology
Movement and Motion
Nuclear physics
Numbers
Nutrition
Organic chemistry
Periodic table
Physics

Plastics
Pollution
Psychology and
　Psychiatry
Resources
Rocks
Seeds
SI Units
Soil
Solar System

Sound
Space exploration
Stars
Statistics
Steam engine
Technology
Veterinary medicine
Virus and Viral diseases
Water
Zoology

Acknowledgments

The publishers would like to thank the following artists for their contribution to this encyclopedia:

Marion Appleton, Craig Austin, Kuo Kang Chen, David Eddington (Maggie Mundy Illustrator's Agency), Dave Etchell, Chris Forsey, Mark Franklin, Jeremy Gower, Hardlines, Hayward Art Group, Christa Hooke (Linden Artists), Lisa Horstman, Industrial Artists, Ian Jackson, John James (Temple Rogers), Felicity Kayes (Design Associates), Elly and Christopher King, Terence Lambert, Steve Latibeaudiere, Mike Long (Design Associates), Chris Lyon, Janos Marffy (Jillian Burgess Agency), William Oliver, David Phipps (Design Associates), Malcolm Porter, Sebastian Quigley (Linden Artists), John Ridyard, Valerie Sangster (Linden Artists), Mike Saunders (Jillian Burgess Agency), George Thompson, John Woodcock (Jillian Burgess Agency), David Wright (Jillian Burgess Agency).

The publishers wish to thank the following for supplying photographs for this encyclopedia:

Cover Science Photo Library (SPL); page 1 SPL; 2 ZEFA; 5 VAG (UK) Ltd (top), Royal Albert Hall (bottom); 7 Paul Brierley; 9 ZEFA; 10 IVECO/Parlour Wood Ltd; 11 ZEFA; 12 SPL; 13 SPL; 15 ZEFA; 17 ZEFA; 18 Derby Museum & Art Gallery; 20 SPL; 21 McDonnell Douglas; 22 ZEFA; 23 SPL (left), ICI (right); 27 Ann Ronan Picture Library; 28 SPL; 29 SPL; 31 Ann Ronan Picture Library; 32 ZEFA; 34 Ronald Grant Archive; 36 Michael Holford (right), Paul Brierley (left); 37 Hutchison Library; 38 ZEFA; 39 SPL; 41 Istanbul University; 44 SPL (right), Grisewood & Dempsey (left); 45 ZEFA; 46 SPL; 48 ZEFA; 50 Science Museum; 51 Grisewood & Dempsey; 52 Mary Evans Picture Library; 53 ZEFA; 54 SPL; 58 ZEFA; 64 ZEFA; 65 SPL; 66 SPL; 67 Mansell Collection (top left), ZEFA (top right), Ann Ronan Picture Library (middle); 68 SPL; 71 F.R.Logan Ltd; 74 ZEFA; 75 SPL; 76 ZEFA (top), SPL (middle) 77 SPL; 78 SPL; 83 SPL; 84 SPL; 85 SPL; 87 ZEFA; 89 Robert Hunt Library (top), ZEFA (bottom); 95 Mike Potts (right), Beech Aircraft Corps (left); 96 Sony (UK) Ltd; 97 ZEFA; 103 Racal-Vodac Ltd; 104 SPL; 106 ZEFA; 108 D.Gardner (left), Isuzu Ceramics Institute (right); 110 SPL; 112 SPL; 115 Terry Cash; 116 Robert Hunt Library (right), ICI Chemicals & Polymers (left); 119 SPL; 120 Life Science Images; 121 SPL; 122 Lucas Film Ltd; 123 ZEFA; 131 ZEFA; 133 ZEFA; 135 NASA; 136 SPL; 139 Science Museum; 140 ZEFA (top), Atlas Copco (bottom); 141 The Moving Picture Co (top and left), Tektronik (UK) Ltd (right); 142 UNISYS; 143 Cray Research Inc; 146 ZEFA; 149 SPL; 151 Michael Hopkins & Partners; 152 ZEFA; 153 ZEFA; 154 ZEFA; 155 Ann Ronan Picture Library; 162 Popperfoto; 163 NASA; 165 National Museum of Photography, Film & Television; 166 Ann Ronan Picture Library (top), Michael Holford (bottom); 169 SPL; 170 SPL; 173 ZEFA; 175 De Beers (right), British Petroleum (left); 180 SPL; 181 ZEFA; 182 House of Seagram; 183 SPL; 185 Ann Ronan Picture Library; 186 SPL; 187 ZEFA; 191 NASA; 193 California Institute of Technology; 197 SPL; 198 Bettmann Archive; 200 PSA; 201 ZEFA; 203 ZEFA; 204 SPL; 209 Cambridge Instruments Ltd; 210 PSA (right), ZEFA (left); 212 Ron Boardman; 214 Herberts; 215 NHPA/M.Tweedie; 218 ZEFA; 220 Paul Brierley; 223 ZEFA; 224 ZEFA; 231 Byrne Photography (right), ZEFA (left); 236 Jet Propulsion Lab, Pasadena, California (left), SPL (right); 239 Canon (UK); 240 Bruce Coleman; 241 NHPA/S.Krasemann; 242 ZEFA; 244 SPL; 245 BTTG; 249 ZEFA; 251 ZEFA; 252 NHPA/D.Woodfall; 253 Ann Ronan Picture Library; 254 ZEFA; 255 ZEFA; 257 Ron Boardman; 259 SPL; 260 SPL; 262 FBI; 263 ZEFA; 264 Dinosaur National Museum, Utah; 265 Ron Boardman; 267 Novosti; 270 Ferodo/ADS Group; 271 SPL; 273 ZEFA; 278 VAG (UK) Ltd; 284 SPL; 285 SPL; 291 SPL; 292 ZEFA; 293 ZEFA; 294 ZEFA; 295 SPL; 296 Johnson Matthey plc; 298 NASA; 307 ZEFA; 308 Bull HN Information Systems; 312 SPL; 313 Allsport; 314 SPL (left), Michael Holford (right); 316 ZEFA; 325 SPL; 326 ZEFA; 329 SPL; 330 SPL; 332 NASA; 334 ZEFA; 336 ZEFA; 337 ZEFA; 339 SPL; 341 SPL; 343 Nestlé; 344 ZEFA; 345 SPL; 350 Science Museum; 351 Transport Road & Research Laboratory; 352 SPL; 354 ZEFA; 355 ICI Group Ltd; 357 ZEFA; 358 Hutchison Library; 359 ZEFA (left), Photographic Services Corp (top), SPL (bottom); 360 NASA; 361 SPL; 362 ZEFA; 363 Shell Research Ltd; 365 Science Museum (top), SPL (bottom); 368 ZEFA; 369 SPL; 370 ZEFA; 373 British Gas plc; 374 MoD; 376 Ron Boardman; 382 SPL; 383 SPL; 385 Beech Aircraft Corps; 386 SPL; 387 ZEFA; 389 ZEFA; 390 NCR (left), ZEFA (right); 391 SPL; 393 Ron Boardman (left), ZEFA (right); 394 ZEFA; 400 ZEFA; 401 ZEFA; 402 SPL; 403 ZEFA (top), SPL (bottom); 406 Casio Electronics Ltd; 412 SPL; 417 British Airways; 418 Ann Ronan Picture Library; 419 SPL; 420 SPL; 422 SPL; 423 SPL; 428 NASA; 430 SPL (left), ZEFA (right); 432 Grisewood & Dempsey; 435 ZEFA; 437 SPL; 440 Biofotos (top), Ron Boardman (bottom); 441 SPL; 443 ZEFA; 444 SPL; 445 SPL; 448 Ron Boardman; 449 Hutchison Library; 450 ZEFA; 452 Ron Boardman; 453 ZEFA; 454 ZEFA; 459 ZEFA; 461 ZEFA; 463 ZEFA; 464 Spectrum Colour Library; 468 Grisewood & Dempsey; 469 Hutchison Library; 470 NASA; 473 ZEFA; 475 ZEFA; 478 SPL; 480 NHPA/M.Tweedie (top), SPL (bottom); 481 ZEFA; 484 SPL; 485 SPL; 486 SPL (left), ZEFA (right); 487 Frank Lane Picture Agency; 489 ICI Explosives; 490 Nobel Foundation; 492 SPL; 494 SPL; 495 SPL; 496 ZEFA; 497 SPL; 501 SPL; 502 SPL; 503 ZEFA; 506 ZEFA; 508 SPL; 509 Ron Boardman; 510 SPL; 511 Science Museum; 512 Paul Brierly (top), SPL (bottom); 513 ZEFA; 514 SPL; 518 ICI Paints; 519 IMITOR; 520 The Hutchison Library; 529 SPL; 531 ICI Chemicals; 533 Ann Ronan Picture Library; 534 IMITOR; 535 Durst; 537 SPL; 541 Terry Cash; 542 SPL; 543 SPL; 544 SPL; 545 Ann Ronan Picture Library; 546 SPL; 547 SPL; 548 ICI Group; 549 ICI Group; 551 Johnson Matthey; 553 UK Atomic Energy Authority Technology; 555 SPL; 556 Polaroid UK; 557 SPL; 558 ZEFA; 559 Exxon Company USA (left), SPL (right); 562 ZEFA (left), SPL (right); 570 Calor Gas Ltd; 571 SPL; 572 Ann Ronan Picture Library (left), ZEFA (right); 573 Mansell Collection; 574 Derek Widdicombe; 575 Pyrex; 577 SPL; 578 SPL; 579 Marconi Co. Ltd; 581 ZEFA; 583 SPL; 585 Polygram; 590 Ann Ronan Picture Library; 591 NHPA/S.Dalton; 592 Frank Lane Picture Agency; 593 NHPA/A.Banninster; 594 ZEFA; 598 ZEFA; 599 ZEFA (top), National Film Archive (bottom), Hunter (left); 600 ZEFA; 601 SPL; 604 Ann Ronan Picture Library (top), ZEFA (bottom); 606 ZEFA; 607 ZEFA; 611 NASA; 612 Science Museum; 613 Biofotos; 616 ZEFA; 619 Ron Boardman; 620 SPL; 621 SPL; 623 NHPA/A.Bannister; 624 ZEFA; 626 Derek Widdicombe; 627 SPL (top), D. Gardner (bottom); 629 ZEFA; 630 ZEFA; 633 SPL; 637 Marconi; 639 Ron Boardman; 641 ZEFA; 643 NASA; 644 NASA; 645 NASA; 647 SPL; 648 NASA; 652 NHPA/S.Krasemann; 653 SPL; 655 ZEFA; 659 Ron Boardman; 661 ZEFA; 663 NHPA/A.Bernard; 665 Ann Ronan Picture Library; 668 Frank Lane Picture Agency (right), SPL (left); 669 SPL; 670 J. Allan Cash; 672 ZEFA; 673 Ron Boardman; 674 ZEFA; 675 SPL; 677 SPL; 679 ZEFA; 680 Ron Boardman; 681 Ron Boardman; 683 Yamaha; 684 Courtaulds Ltd; 685 ZEFA; 691 ZEFA; 692 ZEFA; 693 ZEFA; 694 ZEFA; 695 SPL (top), ZEFA (bottom); 696 ZEFA; 698 SPL; 699 ZEFA; 703 Ron Boardman; 705 ZEFA; 708 MAFF; 709 NHPA/S.Krasemann; 712 J. Allan Cash; 713 ZEFA; 714 ZEFA; 716 CEGB; 718 ZEFA (top), NHPA/G.Bernard (bottom); 720 SPL; 725 Ron Boardman; 726 Ontario Science Centre; 728 ZEFA; 729 SPL; 732 ZEFA (right), J. Allan Cash (left); 734 Sony UK; 735 SPL; 736 Samsung; 737 St. Bartholomew's Hospital; 738 ZEFA; 742 Genet Group; 743 NHPA/D.Woodfall; 744 ZEFA; 746 Panos Pictures; 749 SPL; 750 NHPA/S.Dalton; 753 Mark Edwards/Still Pictures (top), ZEFA (bottom); 755 Dennis Gilbert; 757 SPL (top), British Aerospace (bottom); 758 ZEFA; 761 Musée de l'air; 763 SPL (top), Grisewood & Dempsey (bottom); 764 SPL; 765 SPL; 766 Biofotos; 767 NHPA/M.Leach; 768 SPL.